The Kingdom

A traveller's guide to
the Kingdom of God

Peter
much love. God bless. John
x

The Kingdom

Jesus said: 'Yours is the kingdom' (Matthew 6:13).

John Murfitt

Windsor chair photograph and pen-portrait on the rear cover are the author's.

ISBNs:
Paperback: 978-1-80227-967-2
eBook: 978-1-80227-968-9

British Library Cataloguing-in-Publication Data A catalogue record for this book is available from the British Library.

Contents

Note:

1. References are taken from the New International Version of the Bible, referred to as NIVUK, (The New International Version Anglicised; Biblica; 1978, revised 1984 and 2011).
2. References appear in the familiar format of book, chapter, verse, (as in John 3:16). If already referring to John chapter three, then reference to a verse will be indicated as, for example, (v16). Occasionally there may be reference to KJV: King James Version; 1611. Other versions, where used, will be explained.
3. For conciseness, I have normally referred to the Old Testament as OT and New Testament as NT.
4. Old Testament dating relies on John C. Whitcomb; Old Testament Kings and Prophets; BMH Books; 1977; and: bookshop.org/books/chart-old-testament-kings-and-prophets-paper; 2021. John C. Whitcomb (1924-2020) was professor of theology and Old Testament at Grace Theological Seminary, Winona Lake, Indiana, for 38 years. He is pre-eminent in his field.

This book is dedicated to Ruth, my wife, best friend and fellow citizen in the Kingdom.

Foreword

The United Kingdom, her realms, territories and Common-wealth now has a king: His Majesty King Charles III, but for half of the 20th century and over a fifth of the 21st century, the United Kingdom has been a kingdom ruled by our late queen, Her Majesty Queen Elizabeth II.

While the United Kingdom has featured prominently in world affairs, the Kingdom of God not only embraces the world, but the whole of universal and eternal affairs. The scope and sphere of God's sovereign rule is the Kingdom. The mission and message of Jesus is the Kingdom, and this is the key to the history of our world and the story of humanity leading up to where we are now and on into the future.

The Creator and King, the Messiah and the Mediator of the Kingdom, God's Kingdom, is Jesus. The preaching and teaching of the Kingdom centres on Jesus. While the United Kingdom endures after our monarch, the Kingdom of God is dependent upon the superpower of King Jesus, and he is eternal. Indeed, in global terms, it is his Kingdom which stretches *'from shore to shore, 'til moons shall wax and wane no more'* [ref. Isaac Watts]. There is both a present and a future dimension to this Kingdom and Christian believers should be encouraged to know that this Kingdom can nei-ther be removed nor shaken.

While some scholars maintain that the 'kingdom of God' is clearly distinguished from the 'kingdom of heaven,' this book affirms that they are linguistic variations of the same truth. There are passages in the Bible which use the terms interchangeably while the Gospel writers separately report the same accounts using both terms.

The throne from which the Lord Jesus Christ administers his kingdom is described as a throne of glory, a throne of judgement and a throne of grace. His sceptre is one of righteousness and truth. Though here upon earth, the King wore a crown which had been maliciously constructed with thorns, his present multi-faceted crown proclaims the superiority of his power and the rich glories of all his attributes.

God is the king of his covenant people, who have been purchased by the blood of God's Lion-King, who is also his Lamb-King. According to Revelation chapter 5, he is the only One qualified to break open the mysteries of God's will, because he is the key and the theme of all God's purposes.

While King Solomon was trumpeted as the greatest of kings, and was the one about whose wisdom, wealth and worship the Queen of Sheba commented that 'not even the half was told me' (1 Kings 10:7), yet Jesus proclaimed himself as 'one greater than Solomon' (Luke 11:31). Solomon's kingship and kingdom were the greatest in the estimation of all contemporary world leaders, but Jesus is infinitely greater than Solomon. Jesus, the Son of God, is eternal, independent, holy, all-powerful, all-knowing, ever-present and unchangeable. Jesus has created all things and sustains all things. He forgives the penitent, saves his people, and gives eternal life to the redeemed citizens of his glorious Kingdom.

In the Kingdom of God Jesus reveals that he possesses God's wisdom, God's power, God's knowledge, God's justice, God's faithfulness, God's truthfulness, God's righteousness and God's love. Jesus not only has ownership of divine characteristics and attributes, he possesses 'the fulness of deity' (Colossians 2:9) for Jesus is God Almighty, blessed for ever.

Jesus is the Alpha and Omega, the First and the Last, the King of kings and Lord of lords. He is the exclusive Keyholder of death and Hades. He is sovereign and he rules and reigns for ever over a Kingdom which has no end. He is exceedingly more excellent, more dominant and forever pre-eminent. Jesus' kingship is superior, superlative and supreme. Jesus is the greatest with no equal and no rival so that God's covenant people can confidently proclaim this triumphant truth that 'Our God reigns!'

It is always refreshing to read a book which uses the word of God as its unequivocal and unapologetical foundation. John Murfitt has mined the scriptures, following the valuable vein of the Kingdom, bringing to the surface numerous treasured nuggets which will be of blessing and benefit to the diligent reader. I pray that you will be convinced that 'the Kingdom of God is not a matter of eating and drinking, but of righteousness, peace and joy in the Holy Spirit' (Romans 14:17).

**Geoff Fox, Senior Elder, Haven Church,
Gorran Haven, Cornwall, England, UK.**

Acknowledgements

I would like to say how I have appreciated all that my wife, Ruth, has done to help me prepare this manuscript for publication. She has read my work line by line and made especially useful and helpful suggestions. I am blessed because she understands the theology and has rightly challenged me on numerous occasions and encouraged me to keep going onwards, both in good measure. Furthermore, she has understood when I have spent innumerable hours researching my subject and in writing and revising my manuscript. She has been very long-suffering and I am grateful.

I would also like to sincerely thank Geoff Fox for his invaluable help with certain details and aspects of theology covered in this book. He is a gifted teacher and it is a privilege to receive his teaching. I believe this book is all the richer for his input and I am very grateful for the time he has so willingly given me and for his clarity of understanding and expressing truth found in the Bible. I am particularly grateful for all the time and thought he has put into writing an excellent Foreword for this book. He has carefully and professionally set the scene and raised many of the issues which I have explored and explained in the text. I respect Geoff very much as a special friend and very able theologian and many others also respect him and benefit from his ministry.

In addition, I am grateful to Scott and staff at Publishing Push for their invaluable support and direction to enable this to be a book and not just an idea or a manuscript, and especially to Phil for brilliant proof-reading and editing.

Phil has left no stone unturned and advised me with great skill and attention to detail.

If any mistakes, weaknesses or inaccuracies have slipped through, I take full responsibility for them and I do apologise to you, the reader. I am very blessed indeed, that you have found this book and I thank you, for taking it on to consider its message and reach an informed decision about this vital, thrilling and fascinating subject. May God bless you and may He receive all the praise and glory.

Introduction

In 1952, King George VI (1895-1952) was in poor health so his eldest daughter, Princess Elizabeth, and her husband, Prince Philip, took on his planned visit touring the Commonwealth. In her absence, the King, who had been ill for three years, deteriorated and on Wednesday 6th February 1952, he died unexpectedly in his sleep at Sandringham from pneumonia. A message was sent to Princess Elizabeth, who was in Treetops Hotel in Kenya at the time, that her father had died and that she must quickly return to England. She had become the reigning monarch of The United Kingdom and the British Empire. She immediately prepared to leave Kenya to return home.

As the British legal framework does not allow for a gap in the succession of the reigns of monarchs, and there was no monarch on British soil, the most senior commoner in the Empire was appointed to reign, that is the Lord Mayor of the City of London, so he was appointed as the temporary ruler of the UK and British Empire until the monarch returned.

The position of Lord Mayor dating back to 1189 is an annual appointment and from November 1951 to November 1952 Sir Rupert De La Bere (1893-1978) held the post. He, therefore, became emperor until Princess Elizabeth (1926-2022), as she was when she departed for Kenya, returned as Queen of the *United Kingdom and Commonwealth Realms* on Thursday February 7th.

One of the first things that the uncrowned Queen Elizabeth did was give to Sir Rupert a very ornate scroll thanking him for being the custodian of the Empire for a day. I am privileged to have taken this scroll out of its elaborate case and examined its wording.

When one day Sir Rupert's granddaughter[1] asked me to take for her selected surplus furniture from her home to the rubbish tip, there was a broken chair amongst it, and this was given to me 'for going.' The chair,[2] which belonged to the Lord Mayor, sits on our landing and seeing it afresh after repair has prompted me to think about emperors, queens, and kings, and about empires, realms, and kingdoms. To reflect on one of these, I am reminded that the Bible has much to say about kingdoms, and in particular, *The* Kingdom. Noting that Kingdom means 'king's domain,' all will be revealed as to what the Bible says about this fascinating subject of The Kingdom.

I have grown up with and live in a country with a monarchy and know that most countries of the world do not have a monarchy. I am proud of being British and a citizen of the United Kingdom. At the annual Remembrance Sunday, the media, especially television, is full of the pageantry, pomp and ceremony associated with the day. I have just been watching on television scenes in Whitehall, London on one such occasion showing thousands of military personnel, serving and retired wearing impressive rows of service medals. One medal which is awarded for civil or military service worthy of recognition by 'Crown and Country', is the British Empire Medal first awarded on 24th May 1929. Its inscription is: 'For God, king and country'. Our late Queen was head of State of the United Kingdom and the Commonwealth. It is improper to speak of a queendom, so we had at the time a queen in charge of a kingdom(!), and for 70 years, the UK and Commonwealth have been privileged to have a monarch with an openly positive Christian faith.[3]

We are now privileged to have King Charles III (b.1948), the eldest son of Queen Elizabeth II, as the reigning monarch.

Lewis Carroll (1832-1898) wrote the poem, The Walrus and the Carpenter which begins:

'"The time has come", the Walrus said, "To talk of many things: Of shoes, and ships, and sealing wax, Of cabbages, and kings."'[4]

Kings, Queens and Kingdoms have not only fascinated writers, and often been the subjects of books, they are part of the foundation and fabric of British society. They have also been the subject of hymns because of their great spiritual significance.

Isaac Watts (1674-1748) took part of the OT[5] Psalm 72 and used wording from the NT letter from Paul to the Ephesians in chapter 1 in his famous hymn written in 1719:

'Jesus shall reign where'er the sun, does its successive journeys run; his kingdom spread from shore to shore, till moons shall wax and wane no more.'[6]

I am pleased that Isaac Watts brought together verses from the Old and New Testaments. I also believe both these are utterly reliable, believable and dependable. A close relative and his wife have been missionaries for more than ten years to 'River People' on the Amazon in Brazil. They were a long way upstream but where the river is still a mile wide and where the level rises and falls 30 feet as the seasons change each year. The local people are fishers and are aware of this variation but, because they are dependent on the river for their food and transportation, have three solutions in order to live near the river. The first is that they build high up the banks where they are not affected by the rise and fall of the water. The second is that they build houses on tall stilts. But there is a third way which is fascinating. They build a secure raft which floats on the water whatever its rise or fall and on this raft they build their home. These sometimes have on them a garden and animals. I know from seeing them the rafts are quite large. The base needs to be well constructed to do its job supporting the house, and the house needs a well-constructed base to do its job to keep the family and animals secure. This reminds my relative of the two Testaments, and he explained to me why. The Old Testament is a secure base on which to build the New and the New gives revelation as it reveals the truth from the Old. As the little rhyme attributed to St Augustine of Hippo (354-430), theologian and philosopher, puts it, 'The New is in the Old concealed, the Old is in the New revealed.'

Now, with my mind centred on the truth being accurately conveyed to us through both Testaments by God's Holy Spirit, it is worth questioning what the Bible means when it speaks of *the* kingdom:

Is this physical?
Is it spiritual?
Is it Israel?
Is it heaven?
Who is the king of this kingdom?
Who are the citizens of this kingdom?
Is it something which has developed through the Old Testament, or the New or both?

What is meant by the Old and New Testament references
to it?

Is it the same kingdom in each Testament?

Why is it mentioned at the beginning *and* the end of the
Lord's Prayer?

In fact, why are 473 references to 'kingdom' in the Bible?[7]
Does this indicate its importance?

What is meant in the discussion between Pilate and
Jesus at the trial of Jesus where we read Luke's account: 'So
Pilate asked Jesus, "Are You the **King** of the Jews?" "You have
said so," Jesus replied' (Luke 23:3)? (*Emphasis mine*)

John, the gospel writer and special friend of Jesus, gave
an eye-witness account which is slightly fuller: '"You are
a king then!" said Pilate. Jesus answered. "You say that I am
a king. In fact the reason I was born and came into the world
is to testify to the truth."' (John 18:37) (*Emphasis mine*)[8] [9]

We must also consider verses such as: 'For the kingdom
of God is not a matter of eating and drinking, but of righteousness, peace and joy in the Holy Spirit' (Romans 14:17).

These and other Bible references will be key to our
understanding of what is meant by The Kingdom. It will be
necessary to discover what the Bible says about the physical
kingdom and detail its development for Israel, God's chosen people. It is also important, and more so, to discover
the teaching about the spiritual kingdom for God's chosen
people whom the Bible says are citizens of that kingdom. In
our present self-centred, materialistic age, where materialistic people ignore spiritual things, it will be important to
see what God's plans have been in the past and what plans
he has for the future in relation to the kingdom. I am convinced that God is perfectly fair and just and so each person

has the opportunity to respond to God and his plans. These can be seen worked out looking back into Jewish history, in fulfilment at the time of the writers, and in prophecy looking forward to the future. John Blanchard, writer, evangelist and Christian apologist (1932-2021), reports, 'The British military and political leader Oliver Cromwell (1599-1658) once said,

> "What is history but God's unfolding of himself?" Someone else put it even more succinctly by saying that "History is his story."'[10]

The kingdom of God was one of Jesus' most talked about topics, but it is not a well-understood concept for believers today. If you asked a group of people to define it, you would get a variety of answers. It therefore warrants an investigation into the Bible as our main source of information. The challenge then would be one of how to apply what we find to our lives.

Most scholars think of the kingdom of God as heaven or as the church, and this is partly true. However, the kingdom of God is not an actual physical place. One way to understand God's kingdom and see it from a biblical perspective is to regard it as God's universal reign involving God as Creator and including Christ's exhaustive work as Redeemer. Since God is eternal, his kingdom is eternal. The kingdom of God transcends time and space.

I am thankful and privileged to be able to rely on God's word, the Bible as the primary source of information on the kingdom. As the Apostle Paul told the young pastor, Timothy, 'All Scripture is God-breathed...so that the servant of God may be thoroughly equipped for every good work'

(2 Timothy 3:16). I trust that we will understand God's words and see his plans in the Bible, 'Like apples of gold in settings of silver...' (Proverbs 25:11): as choice fruit in a perfect setting. It will be our challenge and joy to receive them and take them to our hearts, minds, and lives as we live with our knowledge of the kingdom and discover our calling, responding to and obeying the One who calls us.

1   The kingdom in the Old Testament

The word kingdom appears numerous times in the OT, but not as 'kingdom of God.' It appears in phrases such as, '...the kingdom of the Lord ...' (2 Chronicles 13:8) and in the book of Daniel where we read that King Darius of Persia (550-486 BC) recognised '...the living God...and...his kingdom...' (Daniel 6:26). The concept of God's kingship and, therefore, the kingdom, is present throughout the OT and has a clear link with the preaching and teaching of the NT. The OT forms the foundation on which the NT builds. So, we must ask the question, 'What does the OT say about the kingdom of God?' And we discover the most important point is the emphasis that God is king. He is king in two dimensions: spiritually and physically. To understand this better, we are making a journey through the OT, like a train on twin and parallel tracks: the spiritual and the physical.

The spiritual kingdom

Firstly, God is king of the spiritual kingdom. As king his kingdom is the universe. He is king of heaven and earth and of creation. The psalmist wrote, 'The Lord is king for ever and ever; the nations perish from his land' (Psalm 10:16). King Jehoshaphat of Judah (873 – 847 BC) asked, 'O Lord, God of our fathers, are you not the God who is in heaven? You rule over all the kingdoms of the nations' (2 Chronicles 20:6). Another king of Judah was Hezekiah (715-686 BC) who proclaimed, 'Lord Almighty, the God of Israel, enthroned between the cherubim, you alone are God over all the kingdoms of the earth. You have made heaven and earth' (Isaiah 37:16).

In the final book of the OT, God declares through Malachi, (prophesying c436 – 416 BC), '"I am a great king," says the Lord Almighty, "and my name is to be feared among the nations"' (Malachi 1:14). God is the sovereign king in his kingdom: the universe. He delegates power to 'man' (KJV), or 'mankind' (NIVUK) to rule over our part of his kingdom: the Earth. He told Adam and Eve to 'Be fruitful, and increase in number; fill the earth, and subdue it. Rule... over everything' (Genesis 1:28). This commission is re-stated, because of its importance, slightly differently in the next chapter of Genesis: 'The Lord God took the man and put him in the Garden of Eden to work it and take care of it' (Genesis 2:15).

The physical kingdom

Secondly, God is king of the physical kingdom. He is king over Israel in a unique way, and while it is true that God alone is the ultimate king of Israel and over all of creation, human kings have a part to play in this kingdom. In fact, God built human kingship into creation itself. In Genesis chapters 1 and 2, Adam is clearly portrayed as a king in his kingdom. This is observed most clearly in the commission that God gives to him, [11] especially the words 'Then God said, "Let us make mankind in our image, in our likeness, so that they may rule..."' (Genesis 1:26).

Kingship is at the heart of this commission. Adam is to rule over the entire world as a subordinate king under God, the true king over all. Once he had left the Garden of

Eden, he went on to spread God's own dominion outside the boundaries of the ordered garden of Eden to the farthest reaches of creation. In this sense, God reigns over his creation in and through Adam. Sadly, Adam (and Eve) sinned and fell short of God's standard;[12] he failed to take dominion over the earth as God intended. Instead, he rebelled against his own king, the Lord God. Even so, God does not abandon his intention to rule over the earth through people. He decided this because he wanted subjects who would worship him without being forced to do so, as David Pawson (1930-2020), theologian, evangelist and pastor explains,

'They gave him pleasure and he created all things for his pleasure. But he knew that he could never get the same pleasure from beings or creatures that were forced to be his subjects as he would from those who voluntarily said, "We accept your sovereignty."'[13]

The kingdom of Israel develops beginning with Abraham, moving through his descendants and Judges and on to the appointment of kings. The kingdom then splits in two and through the rise of developing warring conquering empires, the Northern and Southern kingdoms of Israel and Judah are conquered and go into exile.[14] Eventually, when Cyrus the Great defeated Babylonia, it suited his purpose and God's for the Jews to return to their own land in 538 BC, and instead of two kingdoms, only one existed: Israel.[15]

At one stage in my teaching life[16] I worked closely with a strongly union-minded Shop Steward. In industry he explained how he and other union colleagues got pay rises for the workers. He told me that if they felt other comparable workers in other industries were getting pay rises then they also deserved a pay rise but negotiating with management was not easy, and pay rises had to be worked at before they were given. They therefore agreed they needed, say, a five percent wage rise and so requested seven percent. The management to save face and not give the workers what they were asking for, offered five percent and the workers showed a grudging acceptance of this, superficially. They had got the rise they wanted, and the management felt they had compromised the rise!

To return to the point of theocracy being replaced by a monarchy, I think this sometimes happens with God's reasoning as well. It is not that he has a plan A and a plan B, but he knows the end from the beginning (Isaiah 46:10), and knows the ultimate outcome is via a plan which appears to fail but leads to the success he has pre-determined, according to Ben Dunson, professor of New Testament at Reformed Theological Seminary in Dallas, Texas.[17]

Theocracy

God's plan for Israel was a theocracy,[18] in Greek, 'the Rule of God,'[19] with God himself as king of the kingdom. He made it clear through Isaiah, 'I am the Lord …your King' (Isaiah 43:15). Israel was not to have an elected president, a monarch, an emperor, or a dictator. It was not to have democracy, autocracy, plutocracy, or any other style of human devised government or leadership. At first all was going quite well with theocracy and God reigning, leading and blessing the nation of Israel and the people accepted God's kingship and reign. Wealthy and successful warrior-leaders led their tribal nomadic people and they became established in a new land. The land, as with the nation, we now call Israel. These patriarchs were followed by judges as the human leaders who acknowledged God's sovereignty and they were raised up by God one by one to lead. Hebrews 11:8-32 lists out-standing nation-founding leaders for their faith including: Abraham, (b. about 2150 BC) Isaac, Jacob, Joseph and Moses. These are followed by judges, including by inference Joshua, (b. about 1355 BC), and named judges including Gideon and Samson.

Judges

In the book of Judges[20] 12 leaders are named as judges, 11 were men and one was a woman called Deborah,[21] but several other leaders in the book may also have been judges. One of the later judges was Samson. He was followed by Eli, who was judge and High Priest. Then came Samuel (1056-1004 BC) who, as prophet and priest, is also regarded as the last judge, '...all the days of his life' (1 Samuel 7:15). (Eli and Samuel were judges but they appear in 1 Samuel).

Monarchy: the first king

However, by the time recorded in 1 Samuel 8, (1021 BC), the Israelites, whose collective faith as a nation was wavering, were so unhappy with Samuel's sons, God as king and judges leading the people that they demanded a human king. They insisted, 'We want a king over us. Then we will be like all the other nations, with a king to lead us and go out before us and fight our battles' (1 Samuel 8:19-20).[22] God gave the people what they wanted, even after Samuel had warned them it was not what God wanted and would lead to problems but they insisted and so had to endure the consequences.[23] The psalmist comments on this sequence of events, 'So he gave them what they asked for, but sent a wasting disease among them' (Psalm 106:15).[24] Samuel responded to God's guidance and anointed Saul (1043 – 1004 BC) as a concession to popular pressure. He was a giant of a man, fit and healthy, with a 'heart' touched by God (1 Samuel 10:9), together with 'valiant men whose heart God had touched' (1 Samuel 10:26).

One of Saul's first successes was to deliver the town of Jabesh Gilead from oppression by the Ammonites. This led to national celebration (1 Samuel 11:15). At this stage he was both humble and a courageous warrior and employed good military strategy as well as dependence on God. However, as he strayed from his faith, God rejected him as king '...and Saul's jealousy of David led to his decline. He died battling the Philistines at Mount Gilboa.'[25]

Monarchy: the second king

Though he began well, Saul failed in his faith and obedience to God and became a failure as a king. He failed to acknowledge God's rule. This led to Samuel, guided again by God, to appoint his successor, David (1004-971 BC), who became ready to reign when Saul ceased to be king. This eventually came about. God *allowed* the first king but then *chose* the second king. (Notice the link to union negotiators mentioned earlier and their demand for a pay rise in a two-part process!)

Through appointment and anointment David was Israel's second king. He proclaimed before all Israel, 'Yours, Lord, is the kingdom; you are exalted as head over all...you are the ruler of all things' (1 Chronicles 29:11b-12a). He was affirming a truth Saul could not that God is the true king and the kingdom belongs to him.

The plan for the kingdom

What we have therefore seen in the OT is the establishment and the development of the kingdom from autocratic and patriarchal beginnings. It is clear in the Bible that God has a plan and that involves his choice of Israel as his special family. He wants *them* to love him as much as *he* loves them. Moses told the people they were to be holy and belonging to the Lord their God who has '...chosen you out of all the peoples on the face of the earth' (Deuteronomy 7:6, and see v7-8), not because they were more numerous or powerful, which they weren't, but because God specially loved them.[26] Because *he* is holy, God requires *them* to be holy and exercise faith and obedience towards him. We then find that people did not necessarily maintain faith, trust and a close relationship with the Lord God and, despite good beginnings, they did not continue to walk closely with him.

From King Saul at the monarchy's beginning through the second king, David, and his son and successor, Solomon, the third king,[27] there was failure to honour and please God in the entire nation of Israel so the Israelites were rejected and sent into exile by God in two main stages: 722 BC and 605 BC.[28] But even in exile, the prophets of Israel predicted that in the last days God would renew his covenant through a Messiah, a righteous Son of David. One of the leading prophets, Jeremiah, referred to this renewal as a new covenant (Jeremiah 31:31). This new covenant would encapsulate God's grace and mercy to his people. He would transform their hearts so that they would obey him and be loyal to him. In return, they would enjoy his unending covenant blessings and would never be rejected again. At the same time, God would act in justice towards all those who opposed him.

God's covenants with David, his successors and the people of Israel were always intended to extend beyond David and Israel. God's reign through David's house was supposed to benefit the entire nation of Israel and Israel's blessings were supposed to benefit the entire world. (Psalms 2, 67; Isaiah 2:2-4; Amos 9:11-15). God's plan was to send a Messiah or Redeemer through David's descendants and that Redeemer would save Israel. This was the importance and centrality of Israel; it was through them that he would rescue all of creation.

God's messengers - the prophets

We have seen that the kingdom went through various phases. It began with a person, Abram (Abraham after his name changed) and straightaway involved his family as they travelled nomadic-like to the promised land. God gave Abram a clear promise about the land 'On that day the Lord made a covenant with Abram and said, "To your descendants I give this land, from the Wadi of Egypt to the great river, the Euphrates"' (Genesis 15:18). The family of Abram became a tribe, and the tribe became a nation. Theocracy, with rule by God, had passed into rule by judges and then into rule by a person, chosen as monarch.

It is worth noting that this aim for the Promised Land has been and remains a focus for Jews throughout the ages. In more recent history, the famous preacher and Civil Rights leader, Rev. Dr. Martin Luther King Jr. (1929-1968) [29] spoke passionately about it as it was embedded in the hearts and minds of God's people in his day and still is now. On one occasion I attended a Passover training day at a synagogue in Wimbledon, London, and heard that orthodox Jews still say at the end of a Passover meal. 'Next year in Israel!'

However, we must consider those of God's people who were appointed for a special task: the prophets. God raised them up to meet the needs of the nation or kingdom. Unlike the priests who represented the people, took their requests and led their worship to God, the prophets represented God and brought his instructions and messages through his messengers to the people.

When the two kingdoms of Israel went into exile the hope for God's rule over the earth in and through a Jewish king (at the time more commonly referred to as an Israelite king) seemed to have come to nothing. As Ben Dunson[30] in his blog reports: the prophets, before during and after the exile however, make it clear that even with the exile God would not and did not, abandon his intention to rule over his people and his world through a king descended from David.

The writings of the prophets show that the only hope for the establishment of an enduring and faithful kingdom in Israel lies in a future work of God we would call redemption. At times there were revivals of faithfulness amongst the population such as in Josiah's reforms (2 Kings 23). But despite Israel's earthly failing leadership, structures and faith in organising the kingdom, God still did not abandon his plan to reign over the world through his appointed human king.

Isaiah[31]

Together with Jeremiah and Ezekiel, Isaiah is a leading 'former' or 'major' prophet. With the people despondent in exile, the question to consider is 'How will this reign come about?' Isaiah, for instance, said that God would come in power to rescue and restore his people: 'They will see the glory of the Lord ...your God will come...he will come to save you...They will enter Zion (*Jerusalem*) with singing' (Isaiah 35:1-4, 8-10).[32] (*Emphasis mine*)

God had not stopped being king simply because of the failure of Israel's earthly kings. Instead, speaking of a return of the Jews from exile to the Promised Land, God's physical kingdom, God in his grace and mercy would bring salvation and rescue for his erring and faithless people. Isaiah explained that in the future if the kingdom of God is to be clearly seen across the earth and if Israel is to be a light to the nations, it will be brought about through a messianic, redeeming king. This is also seen in further prophecies by Isaiah (Isaiah 9:1-7; 42:1-9).

Isaiah gives words of real encouragement and challenge to the people,

'How beautiful on the mountains are the feet of those who bring good news, who proclaim peace, who brings good tidings, who proclaim salvation, who say to Zion, "Your God reigns!" Listen! Your watchmen lift up their voices; together they shout for joy. When the Lord returns to Zion, they will see it with their own eyes. Burst into songs of joy together, you ruins of Jerusalem, for the Lord has comforted his people, he has redeemed Jerusalem. The Lord will lay bare his holy arm in the sight of all the nations, and all the ends of the earth will see the salvation of our God' (Isaiah 52:7-10).

Isaiah further speaks of a coming servant of the Lord who '...will be raised and lifted up and highly exalted' (Isaiah 52:13). This is the language of kingly exaltation; that of a Messiah or Redeemer. This is both a forthtelling of imminent action to meet present circumstances and a foretelling of the Redeemer to come: Jesus.

Jeremiah[33]

Jeremiah expresses the same rescue and redemption with the imagery of God placing shepherds[34] over His people in the context of bringing them out from the nations to which they have been driven. God says,

> '"I myself will gather the remnant of my flock out of all the countries where I have driven them and will bring them back to their pasture, where they will be fruitful and increase in number. I will place shepherds over them who will tend them, and they will no longer be afraid or terrified, nor will any be missing" declares the Lord' (Jeremiah 23:3-4).

Daniel[35]

Daniel is a man of faith and a devout Jew exiled in a foreign land, but he is both close to God and became close to Nebuchadnezzar (605-562 BC), King of Babylon. With his God-given gift of interpreting dreams, he was able to tell the king what he dreamed (because the king could not at first remember). He described a statue and gave its interpretation. He spoke of kings and kingdoms but went on to say what would eventually happen. 'In the time of those kings, the God of heaven will set up a kingdom that will never be destroyed, nor will it be left to another people. It will crush all those kingdoms and bring them to an end, but it will itself endure forever' (Daniel 2:44).

Daniel, who years later was still in exile, found himself in the reign of a new king and this time it was he who has a dream of Four Beasts. We read,

'In the first year of Belshazzar[36] king of Babylon, Daniel had a dream and visions passed through his mind as he was lying in bed. He wrote down the substance of his dream' (Daniel 7:1).

'In my vision at night I looked, and there before me was one like a son of man, coming with the clouds of heaven. He approached the Ancient of Days and was led into his presence. He was given authority, glory and sovereign power; all nations and peoples of every language worshipped him. His dominion is an everlasting dominion that will not pass away, and his kingdom is one that will never be destroyed' (Daniel 7:13-14).

Daniel is part of the Hagiographa, or 'writings' used to encourage persecuted Jews in the second century BC, but is considered by some scholars to be a prophet because of the prophetic content of his book. He addresses both the present and the future as with the leading prophets. In the time of the exile, God promised to establish his kingdom over all nations, both then and in the future through the Son of Man (as in Daniel 7). This will be a kingdom that would never pass away or be destroyed. The commission given to Adam will be fulfilled. Through the ultimate king, Jesus, God would establish his kingdom over all peoples. Daniel prophesied that God would enact judgment on sin and inferior kingdoms 'in favour of the holy people of the Most High (*God*) and the time came when they possessed the kingdom' (Daniel 7:22). (*Emphasis mine*)

After 70 years Israel returns from its exile in Babylon but the reports in Ezra and Nehemiah of their return fall short of the prophetic hope of a renewed Israel ruled over by a righteous king and descendant of David. God '...moved the heart of Cyrus king of Persia' (550-530 BC) (2 Chronicles 36:22) to send the Israelites back to Jerusalem to rebuild their temple, which they did (Ezra 1-6), but Israel doesn't achieve the glory of the monarchy experienced under King David. This is seen most clearly in the weeping of the elders of the people at the dedication of the new temple since it falls short of the glory of the previous temple (Ezra 3:12-13). Older Jews present remembered the first temple before it was destroyed by the conquering Babylonians in 722 BC.

Kingship in prophecy

While the prophets consistently speak of God as the one who in sovereignty will ensure his spiritual kingdom is firmly and totally established, they also speak of this as being accomplished through a kingly Messiah. This Messiah is described in significant statements in the prophets, but two passages stand out as being particularly important for our understanding of the king and the kingdom: Isaiah 9 and Daniel 7.

As I write it is the Christmas season and I am constantly reminded of words used in appropriate Christian literature and songs. We hear the words, 'For to us a child is born, to us a son is given, and the government will be on his shoulders' (Isaiah 9:6a).[37] Then we meet the dramatic words of v7, 'Of the greatness of his government and peace there will be no end. He will reign on David's throne and over his *kingdom*, establishing and upholding it with justice and righteousness from that time on and for ever. The zeal of the Lord Almighty will accomplish this.' (*Emphasis mine*)

In Daniel 7 the coming kingly deliverer of God's people is '...given authority, glory and sovereign power...His dominion is an everlasting dominion that will not pass away, and his kingdom is one that will never be destroyed' (Daniel 7:14). King Belshazzar of Babylon was reigning under the authority of God and as Daniel reflected on his own 'vision' (v13) and its interpretation, he said, 'I, Daniel was troubled in spirit, and the visions that passed through my mind disturbed me' (v15). He was then told by an onlooker standing by the statue, 'But the holy people of the Most High will receive *the kingdom* and will possess it forever – yes, for ever and ever' (v18). (*Emphasis mine*) This leads to v22 in which God's people possess this kingdom.

These two Important passages of Isaiah 9 and Daniel 7 speak of the establishment of the kingdom, of God reigning over it, Jesus being the king of the kingdom and his people possessing it. This is what victory looks like in the future but brought about through the suffering of Jesus, God's king, as Isaiah makes plain in calling him a 'man of suffering'... '...and the will of the Lord will prosper in his hand' (Isaiah 53:3, v10b). This was difficult for many Jews to accept at the time spoken and later during the ministry of Jesus where we read, 'Jesus knowing that they intended to come and make him king by force, withdrew again to a mountain by himself'

(John 6:15). As Ben Dunson[38] explains, The Jews expected a triumphant king, without understanding how he would triumph.

God did not give up on his wayward people or in acting with grace and mercy, but he required of the people, obedience, led by their king, and an undivided heart of faith on the part of the people of Israel. Sadly, Saul fell short, but not David. Despite all of David's failings, he longed to please God and was so sorry when he let him down, (Psalm 51, especially v1-3). Under David's leadership and God's sovereignty, the physical kingdom was firmly established.

The spiritual kingdom had its roots in Eden and in God's plans for all of creation. Throughout the OT days, though, it was only understood by a minority of the Jewish nation that God's desire was to be the king of a spiritual kingdom. Most people still looked for a physical kingdom. This continues to be the case as we explore the reaction to the teaching of Jesus in the NT and as we see the teaching of the first Christians.

I trust as we leave behind the physical kingdom linked with the spiritual kingdom, like the two rails of the train track and concentrate just on the spiritual kingdom, we will catch a glimpse of the kingdom as it was taught in NT days and move on into the future until the end of the age when the king returns. If we continue the analogy at the beginning of this chapter of a train travelling on twin rails, we must now move on to a single rail: a monorail! This is explored in the next chapter and explained further at the start of chapter three where we see Jesus involved in one-to-one witness and healing, and so gives a living example of the spiritual kingdom.

2 | The kingdom in the New Testament.

Hallelujah

One of my favourite pieces of music is the Hallelujah Chorus in Handel's[39] Messiah. In public performances there is now a tradition to stand during this piece in the oratorio. The generally accepted reason is that King George II (1683-1760) stood up during the chorus at the 1743 London premiere at Covent Garden to show his reverence towards God as supreme King. Since it was considered good etiquette to do what the king did the audience followed. The text for the chorus comes from Revelation: '...the Lord God omnipotent reigneth...King of kings and Lord of lords...and he shall reign for ever and ever' (Revelation 19:6, v16; 11:15 KJV). Handel was showing his faith as well as his great ability in putting great truths to great music. He knew he was a herald in that sense as he expressed through his music the kingdom which was, is and was yet to come in all its fullness and glory. This sets our scene well for our study of the kingdom as found in the NT.

The concept of God's kingship, as seen in the last chapter, is present throughout the OT and it is particularly important to see the spiritual dimension if we are going to make sense of Jesus' preaching about the kingdom of God. Just prior to Jesus' ministry his cousin, John the Baptist, appeared in ministry. As Jesus was leaving his craft as a

carpenter and builder, so John was leaving his family to proclaim Jesus as the promised Messiah and to prepare people
to meet him. So, as a herald he addressed all sections of his
audience '...saying, "Repent for the kingdom of heaven has
come near"'(NIVUK), or "...is at hand"' (KJV) (Matthew 3:2).
John knew that His hearers had a grasp of what he meant,
even if he knew that they did not fully understand. His role
was not to convince but to warn and challenge.[40] John the
Baptist is regarded as the last OT prophet.

The word Kingdom appears 162 times in the NT.[41]
Another interesting fact is that The Kingdom of Heaven
appears 32 of these times in the Gospel of Matthew. Only
Matthew expresses it like this in the NT.[42] It is also a fact
that there are more than 300 prophecies in the OT speaking
of the Messiah to come. They were all fulfilled, amazingly, in
the precise details of the birth, life, death, resurrection and
ascension of Jesus.

The Messiah comes into Simeon's life

The prophets looked to the future and the coming of the
Messiah to establish his kingdom and they looked to a future
day when God would come in power to set it up. Behind the
scenes God planned to come to earth, as God (John 1:1-14),
and as a perfect human being. There must have been a conversation between the Son and the Father in heaven ahead
of his coming about what form he should take because in
Hebrews we read, '...when Christ came into the world, he
said: "Sacrifice and offering you did not desire, but a body
you prepared for me;" ..."Then I said, 'Here I am – it is written...I have come to do your will, my God'" (Hebrews 10:5,
v7). It is with this sense of anticipation that the Gospels

such as Luke opens. There we are introduced to Simeon, who speaks as a prophet, looking for the coming kingdom: he expects this to happen before he dies. We read,

> 'Now there was a man in Jerusalem called Simeon, who was righteous and devout. He was waiting for the consolation of Israel, and the Holy Spirit was on him. It had been revealed to him by the Holy Spirit that he would not die before he had seen the Lord's Messiah. Moved by the Spirit, he went into the temple courts. When the parents brought in the child Jesus to do for him what the custom of the law required, Simeon took him in his arms and praised God, saying, "Sovereign Lord, as you have promised, you may now dismiss your servant in peace. For my eyes have seen your salvation, which you have prepared in the sight of all nations: a light for revelation to the Gentiles, and the glory of your people Israel"' (Luke 2:25-32).

The Messiah comes into a political situation

There were two groups of people in the political situation of the Jewish Roman world awaiting redemption in Jerusalem. The first group were those, like the elderly prophets: Simeon, who lived in a house in Jerusalem, Anna, who lived in the temple, and some others who got on with their everyday lives but had spiritual insight, who were waiting for spiritual redemption (Luke 2:38). The second group were those who were waiting for Jerusalem to be freed from Roman occupation by military intervention. Both groups knew that a king would one day come who would save and deliver God's people, though this was understood differently by the two groups. RC Sproul (1939-2017), an American Reformed theologian, founder of Ligonier Ministries, and former ordained pastor of Saint Andrew's Chapel (Presbyterian) in Sanford, Florida, comments,

> 'The Old Testament teaching on God's kingdom is the necessary context for making sense of Jesus' teaching and preaching, especially his announcement that the kingdom of God was "at hand"' (Matthew 3:2 KJV).[43]

Many Jews Jesus preached to knew that God was and always had been king. Others did not see things this way. They failed to grasp that the presence of Jesus was the coming of God's kingdom in a unique way and that his ministry was the preparation for the final days predicted by the prophets. The establishment by Jesus of his spiritual kingdom happened; freeing the Jewish nation from Roman occupation did not happen.

The kingdom in the Synoptic Gospels[44]

As a simple statement of fact a kingdom is where a king reigns and it embodies the territory over which he reigns. I believe that since God is the Creator of everything, the extent of his realm must be the whole universe, but within the scope of our study, we concentrate on the world. Therefore, as the kingdom of God is wherever God reigns, and since he reigns everywhere, the kingdom of God is everywhere.

To look at the kingdom within the pages of the NT, we see John the Baptist coming out of the wilderness with his urgent call, 'Repent, for the kingdom of God is at hand' (ESV),[45] 'has come near' (NIVUK), or ''The kingdom of heaven is at hand' (KJV), (Matthew 3:2). This same message was repeated by Jesus when he started his ministry: 'From that time on Jesus began to preach, "Repent, for the kingdom of heaven has come near"' (Matthew 4:17).

The Messianic King

Most people recognise Hampton Court Palace. It is a Grade I listed royal palace in Richmond, London. The construction of the palace began in 1514 as a rather splendid home for Cardinal Thomas Wolsey (1473-1530), the chief minister of King Henry VIII (1491-1547). In 1529, as Wolsey fell from favour, the cardinal was obliged to give the palace to the king to try and cancel his fall from grace and appease the king. The palace went on to become one of Henry's most favoured residences and soon after acquiring the property, he enlarged it to better accommodate his vast retinue of courtiers. Along with St James' Palace, it is one of only two surviving palaces out of the many the king owned. The palace is currently in the possession of the Crown. On one occasion I had the opportunity of a private visit to meet and 'shadow' the Chief Executive who managed the estate and I had an insight as to what happened on a daily basis, including the finances, and had a look behind the scenes and toured the areas not open to the public.

Our tour of the NT is an insight into how God sees the need for the messianic kingdom. We have the opportunity to see behind the scenes of our lives involving a nation with royalty, political leaders, health and education specialists, and those who lead us in business, finance and worship as in the fabric of this country. So many things are highly visible. It is the same but more splendid with God's hand in creation and sustenance of life, and behind the obvious he is unveiling his kingdom. Our lives are built on past experience and we have the privilege and opportunity to shape the future. We find truth emerging and that the kingdom of God is a kingdom that will be ruled by God's appointed Messiah who will be not just the Redeemer of his people, but the King reigning over his kingdom. John the Baptist had therefore, been granted an insight to understand that the coming kingdom was the kingdom of the Messiah. This naturally means that by the start of the ministry of John and Jesus, both as Jews at the recognised authoritative rabbinic age of 30, John had put on one side the fact that humanly speaking, they were cousins. They were both moving forward in unique roles to reveal the kingdom of God. John, the last in a lengthy line of OT prophets, prepared the way and Jesus built on this to show God's love and fulfil his mission as the Messiah, the Saviour, the Redeemer of the world.

Towards the end of Jesus' life on earth, just as he was about to return to his father in heaven, his disciples had the opportunity to ask him one last question, 'Lord, will You at this time restore the kingdom to Israel?' (Acts 1:6). They still had not understood the kingdom in Jesus' ministry as a spiritual kingdom and still thought he could be a victorious king, with human military resources, in the style of King David. Their assumption was that he would overthrow the Roman occupation. It was three years earlier that this was expressed by the ordinary people who were amazed at his feeding of the 5,000[46] as explained earlier. They wanted to take him by force and make him king. The answer of Jesus was patient and gracious. 'He said to them: "It is not for you to know times or dates which the Father has set by his own authority"' (Acts 1:7).

The King on trial

During his interrogation Jesus told Pilate, '" My kingdom is not of this world. If it were, my servants would fight to prevent my arrest by the Jewish leaders. But now my kingdom is from another place." "You are a king, then!" said Pilate' (John 18:36-37). Jesus agreed and was saying that his kingdom was spiritual, indicating that it was a kingdom in the hearts of those who trusted him as their Saviour or Messiah. With the benefit of hindsight, we can look back at the OT and see this kingdom promised that would be in people's hearts, ruled by God's anointed Messiah. This was not the physical kingdom the people wanted him for: to take and lead by force. To the discerning in his earthly ministry, Jesus made this clear, 'If I drive out demons by the finger of God, then the kingdom of God has come upon you' (Luke 11:20). In Luke chapter 10 we read that in the sending out of the disciples, Jesus told the 70 that if a town welcomes them, he said,

> 'Heal those there who are ill and tell them, "The kingdom of God has come near to you. But when you enter a town and are not welcomed, go into its streets and say, Even the dust of your town we wipe from our feet as a warning to you. Yet be sure of this: the kingdom of God has come near"' (Luke 10:9-11).

If we ask the question, 'How could the kingdom of God be near them?' The answer must be that the kingdom of God was near to them because the King of the kingdom was there. His kingdom had begun on earth and Jesus would ultimately be 'King of kings and Lord of lords' (Revelation 19:16) at the end of the age; glorious words used by Handel in his oratorio.

So, Jesus' kingship is not something only consigned to the future. Jesus is King right now. All authority in heaven and on earth has been given by God to his anointed Son; the Messiah; the King. (Matthew 28:18).

Citizenship

I have been privileged to visit countries on three continents. On one occasion I visited Victoria on Vancouver Island, Canada and went to a very English looking restaurant. There, as with other countries I have visited, I was proud to say, when asked, that I was British. When a waitress asked where in England was I from, and I said I was from Kent, her eyes lit up and she replied, 'Do you by any chance know John Smith (or some similar name) who lives in Kent?' I was quite amused by this and said I didn't. I was thinking that Kent was 1400 square miles and had a population at the time of just less than two million. I am proud to be a citizen of the United Kingdom but was also pleased to be a temporary citizen of and visitor to Canada.

I can equally be a citizen of the United Kingdom and also a citizen of the kingdom of heaven, without there being any conflict. The first is physical and temporary, the second is spiritual and eternal. As Easton's Bible Dictionary puts it:

'We experience the challenge of the citizenship of heaven when Jesus tells us to pray, "Your kingdom come..." (Matthew 6:10).'[47]

The kingdom in the Gospel of John

The Gospel of John has only two references to the kingdom of God: in chapters 3 and 18. This is because the theological emphases John has chosen throughout his gospel is the deity of Christ and salvation through him. He does, however, mention frequently a concept parallel to the kingdom: eternal life.

In John 3 Jesus raised the subject of the kingdom with his visitor, Nicodemus, linking it with the new birth.[48] Jesus said that Just as we are born in the flesh, so we must also be born in the spirit in order to enter the kingdom of God and told Nicodemus, 'Very truly I tell you, no one can see the kingdom of God unless they are born again' (John 3:3). He had in mind both the present spiritual form of the kingdom and his future earthly reign. He was making it clear it is impossible to enter the kingdom of God without the new birth and showed surprise at Nicodemus not understanding this OT concept.[49]

The only other reference to the kingdom in the Gospel of John is found in chapter 18, as already discussed in the trial of Jesus before Pilate, (John 18:36-37). John Walvoord, President of Dallas Theological Seminary writes in 2008,

> 'Christ indicated that his kingdom did not receive its power from the world which relies on physical force for its endurance. Whether referring to the present physical form of the kingdom or the future millennial kingdom, Christ's statement would be true in either case.'[50]

John indicates that Jesus clearly offered a present form of the kingdom which believers can enter now by new birth. Walvoord concluded:

'He also reaffirmed the hope of the Jews that there would be a future kingdom in which the Son of David will reign over the House of Israel.'[51]

The kingdom in Acts

The Book of Acts begins and ends with the kingdom of God. Luke begins the book by giving his promise of accurate content as he writes to Theophilus,[52] a person of standing whom Luke informs, according to scholars, as his friend. He reported to him how Jesus, risen from the dead, appeared to the disciples, '...and gave many convincing proofs that he was alive. He appeared to them over a period of forty days[53] and spoke about the kingdom of God' (Acts 1:3b). Jesus wanted the disciples to be confident about the kingdom, explaining to them every part of their Scriptures[54] (we call the OT); Luke wants the same for his readers. Jesus taught them by example and instructed them that during this momentous time of preparation for local and world mission, they must be sure to speak of the kingdom of God. They longed to see the divided kingdom, made up of Judea and Samaria united, more under the Messiah's rule and free from the oppressive rule of Rome. The disciples may have hoped that the reign of Jesus would mean that Caesar would no longer rule over Jerusalem or Israel and its near neighbours.

Acts ends with the apostle Paul in the heart of Rome, the capital city of the Roman Empire. There, 'He proclaimed the kingdom of God and taught about the Lord Jesus Christ – with all boldness and without hindrance!' (Acts 28:31)

To return to the beginning

Luke begins Acts by telling his friend, 'In my former book, Theophilus, I wrote about all that Jesus began to do and to teach' (Acts 1:1). This second book is all that Jesus continued to do and to teach through the Holy Spirit who now makes his presence and power known through the apostles and the early Christian communities. The kingdom is a central theme but is not mentioned as frequently as in Luke's gospel. The word *kingdom* occurs 42 times in Luke but just eight times in Acts. Five of these references occur in the context of *preaching the kingdom*. The kingdom is coming in its fullness at the end of time. When Luke wrote, the reality of the kingdom could only be experienced through repentance and faith.

To give a firm footing for the preaching and teaching in Acts, we must first recap briefly on the foundation laid by the OT prophets who not only foretold the future, as inspired by God, but they also longed for the day when God's kingdom would be established. 'In the time of those kings[55] the God of heaven will set up a kingdom that will never be destroyed, nor will it be left to another people. It will crush all those kingdoms and bring them to an end, but it will itself endure forever' (Daniel 2:44). This was the promise God made to David to establish his royal dynasty, 'I will establish the throne of his kingdom forever' (2 Samuel 7:13b). These royal kingdom prospects were deeply intertwined with Israel's national prospects. By the end of the OT Second book of Kings, the nation was carried off into exile together with Israel's last king Zedekiah, in chains (Jeremiah 34:21). But the prophets saw a glorious future in which the nation and the royal lineage of David and the kingdom would be restored (Isaiah 9:6-7; 55:3). So, when the apostles asked Jesus at the start of Acts about restoring the kingdom to Israel (Acts 1:6), Jesus pointed out that God had planned to restore the nation in his own time and in his own way, and would use the restoration to draw all people to himself (Isaiah 2:2-4). This preaching and teaching was intended to move them in their understanding from the physical to the spiritual kingdom.

Later, on the day of Pentecost, Peter, with inner understanding given by God the Holy Spirit, addressed the crowd and said this outpouring of the Holy Spirit signalled that the long-awaited plan of God had commenced (Acts 2:14-21). As the book of Acts unfolds, God's plan was revealed and it became clear to those with insight that it was a spiritual kingdom that had begun, and was to be entered by faith through God's grace and by people being saved from their sin. As Paul said, 'Everyone who calls on the name of the Lord will be saved' (Romans 10:13). There is no alternative way. None was needed. God's plan was sufficient. Everyone then and since can partake of this provision by faith through grace. As Arthur Bliss (1838-1876), a hymn-writing, singing evangelist, wrote in his joyful hymn, 'Whosoever will may come.'[56]

Moving out with the Apostles

In Acts and the NT Epistles the emphasis continues to be on finding citizens for the kingdom. It is as if Jesus was saying now you have the Holy Spirit in you, you must go anywhere and everywhere I send you: what you are really looking for are people to bring into the kingdom.

The Holy Spirit was at work encouraging and guiding individuals during the early days of persecution after Jesus had ascended to heaven. On one particular day Philip travelled away from Jerusalem, where he was with Christians standing firm in their faith, and '...went down to a city in Samaria and...proclaimed the good news of the kingdom of God' (Acts 8:5, v12). He and the other Apostles were sure restoration was coming and people were being accepted into God's kingdom by faith, whether Jews or Gentiles, and whether circumcised or not. The days of Acts were dramatic days as individuals called on the name of the Lord to be saved, and in doing so from the heart, they were born again and admitted into the kingdom.

This is the message of the gospel and kingdom in Acts and there we see life-changing events. The message is actually the story that the world's true king is not Caesar but Christ and that the citizenship that counts is not identity as a Roman but as a Christian. It is these early converts to Christianity who were fired up with the message of the kingdom and we read what happened when two of them, Paul and Silas, went to Thessalonica and preached boldly in the synagogue there. Some Jews present took great exception to this and said,

'These men who have caused trouble all over the world have now come here, and Jason has welcomed them into his house. They are all defying Caesar's decrees, saying that there is another king, one called Jesus' (Acts 17:6-7).

The Jews in Ephesus were also challenged by Paul speaking about the kingdom for an extended period, 'Paul entered the synagogue and spoke boldly there for three months, arguing persuasively about the kingdom of God' (Acts 19:8).[57] Sadly, in his farewell speech in which he tells his audience they would never see him again (Acts 20:38), on the beach at Miletus, Paul reminded the Ephesian elders how he had gone among them preaching the kingdom and thus proclaiming to them 'the whole will of God' ('...counsel of God.' KJV) (Acts 20:27). (See a fuller statement in Acts 20:25-27).

In Acts the ministry of the kingdom involves teaching, preaching and healing, pioneer evangelism, disciple making, church planting and church strengthening. There is also a future element to the kingdom and disciples must persevere to enter the kingdom.

As Chris Green, a researcher at Oxford University, puts it:

'When Paul and Barnabas preached the gospel, made many new disciples and planted churches on their first missionary journey, they returned to strengthen the disciples and remind them that, "We must go through many hardships to enter the kingdom of God"' (Acts 14:22b).[58]

Looking to the future

Even in his house-arrest imprisonment for two years at the end of Acts, Paul was still preaching fearlessly at every opportunity (Acts 28:17-31). He 'witnessed to them from morning till evening, explaining about the kingdom of God, and from the Law of Moses and from the Prophets he tried to persuade them about Jesus' (v23).

With this example of boldness, Shane Scott, a Minister for the Church of Christ, Valrico, Florida adds,

'Be emboldened as a follower of the Lord to proclaim the gospel of the kingdom.'[59]

Ian Paul, theologian and author, Associate Minister of St Nicholas Nottingham, UK, also comments on Acts,

> 'Luke seems to imagine that there is a continuing Chapter 29 – in which successive generations of Christians continue the teaching and wonderful signs done by Jesus. We are invited to be collaborators in the kingdom of God with him.'[60]

The teaching and preaching of the kingdom in Acts lead to dramatic consequences, and so Chris Green concludes that,

> 'It (*the kingdom*) cannot be separated from the risen King who rules from heaven. Jesus is in heaven, but he is not absent from earth. He is the active ruler over his kingdom. The building and equipping of his church are exactly what his kingly rule is designed to produce until his return in glory.'[61] (*Emphasis mine*)

One final thought about the kingdom in Acts is from Living Stream Ministry who assert,

> 'Some theologians believe that the kingdom has been suspended due to the rejection of the Jews. They believe that this is not the kingdom age, but the church age and that the kingdom will come later on. This teaching is incorrect. Even in this age, the age of grace, the kingdom is here.'[62]

The kingdom in the Epistles

References to the kingdom are frequently found in the letters we call the Epistles. According to RH Boll (1875-1956) a German-born American preacher in the Churches of Christ, tells us that the Epistles,

> '...present the kingdom as now present in spiritual manifestation, and also as future in outward manifestation and its future world-rule, just as we have seen it in the Gospels and Acts.'[63]

The nature of that spiritual, '...heavenly kingdom...' (2 Timothy 4:18) and rule, and the part played by believers in it, is revealed in a number of NT references. It is a 'heavenly kingdom,' and the king of it rules over the earth, but it is also the '...world to come...' (Hebrews 2:5). Boll tells us it is literally in the Greek,

> 'The inhabited earth to come.'[64]

This kingdom is to be governed by people as God had originally planned, 'Then God said, "Let us make mankind in our image, in our likeness, so that they may rule..."' (Genesis 1:26a). God reigns as king and people who are saved by grace through faith are privileged to rule with him. The kingdom, the whole creation, Paul sees as awaiting eagerly to be liberated, '...from its bondage to decay and brought into the freedom and glory of the children of God' (Romans 8:21). This is the kingdom we are discovering.

Those who are in and those who are out of the kingdom

The Epistles continue from the gospels and Acts as they tell us that the believers have been '...brought into the kingdom of the Son he loves' (Colossians 1:13). This is, 'A kingdom that cannot be shaken...' (Hebrews 12:28). The kingdom of Christ, filled with God's love into which we are accepted by grace, is the realm in which the Lord Jesus Christ exercises his kingship and rule. In it is where the believers have their citizenship. The seat of its authority and government is heaven; therefore Paul tells us that '...our citizenship is in heaven' (Philippians 3:20). The essential spiritual features of this kingdom are '...righteousness,[65] peace, and joy in the Holy Spirit' (Romans 14:17). Paul makes it clear in his epistle to the Corinthian church that certain members have become arrogant and are doing too much 'talking' and says, 'The kingdom of God is not a matter of talk but of power' (1 Corinthians 4:18-20). Paul has to point out to the Corinthians that those who fail morally, such as 'wrongdoers... the sexually immoral... idolators... adulterers... men who have sex with men... thieves... the greedy... drunkards... slanderers... swindlers will (not) inherit the kingdom of God' (1 Corinthians 6:9-12). (*Insertion mine*)

The Epistles also show that a number of the believers were Paul's fellow workers in sharing the gospel and kingdom including Tychicus, Onesimus, Aristarchus, Mark and Jesus Justus. They were '...fellow workers for the kingdom of God' (Colossians 4:11). He further points out that '...flesh and blood cannot inherit the kingdom of God' (1 Corinthians 15:50). And with the Galatians, he counsels that those who perform 'The acts of the flesh...will not inherit the kingdom of God' (Galatians 5:19, v21). He is equally firm with the Ephesians telling them, 'For of this you can be sure: no immoral, impure or greedy person...has any inheritance in the kingdom of Christ and of God' (Ephesians 5:5). To the Thessalonians he says they must live '...worthy of God, who calls you into his kingdom and glory' (1 Thessalonians 2:12).

James, brother of Jesus

James, stepbrother of Jesus and leader of the Jerusalem church, is also challenging his Christian brothers and sisters: '...has not God chosen those who are poor in the eyes of the world to be rich in faith and to inherit the kingdom he promised those who love him?' (James 2:5)

Peter, friend of Jesus

Peter, the outspoken fisherman and special friend of Jesus, declared to the readers of his first letter, 'Therefore my brothers and sisters, make every effort to confirm your calling and election...and you will receive a rich welcome into the eternal kingdom of our Lord and Saviour Jesus Christ' (2 Peter 1:10-11). This is why Peter tells us that within this kingdom we will be, '...receiving the goal of your faith, the salvation of your souls' (1 Peter 1:9).

The kingdom present and future

In the future kingdom Christians will judge the world (1 Corinthians 6:2), and we are told 'If we endure, we will also reign with him' (2 Timothy 2:12), and will be 'crowned' (2 Timothy 4:8) with Jesus our Saviour and king. There are certainly wonderful things to look forward to in the kingdom present and future as shown in the Epistles.

The kingdom in Revelation

We now arrive at the kingdom in all its glory, complexity and beauty as unveiled in the book of Revelation.[66] I believe this was written under divine inspiration by John the Apostle, (Revelation 1:4) (accepted by most scholars as the writer of the gospel and letters also bearing his name), John the elder, (according to second century Christian writers – Papias, Justin Martyr, Irenaeus, and others),[67] or St. John the Divine (as the title appears in Revelation, KJV). As Genesis and Revelation are like the two book ends of a wonderful collection of a 66-book library, including the two ends, we must conclude that they contain all that God has 'breathed' (2 Timothy 3:16) into their pages for our salvation. They give us the knowledge of God he wishes us to have and knowledge of human life in all its variety and richness, successes and failures. Revelation rounds off the Bible in general and NT in particular and gives the final essential information we need for our studies of the kingdom.

John sets the scene

John, in his scene-setting introduction to Revelation, said he was a brother and companion with the believers in the '...kingdom and patient endurance in Jesus' (Revelation 1:9). The kingdom is both now and for the future and so must the patient endurance be. John was in the kingdom at that time of writing, and I and other Christians are in the kingdom right now. Other citizens of the kingdom are yet to be born. The Chinese Christian preacher and hymn-writer in Taiwan, Witness Lee (1905-1997), tells us,

> 'This kingdom present now, will come in its full manifestation after the great tribulation.'[68]

The kingdom has come

So, we read the words revealed to John, '...The kingdom of the world has become the kingdom of our Lord and of his Messiah' (Revelation 11:15b).

We see God as a powerful and reigning king and believers as '...his kingdom and priests who serve God his father...' in John's greeting to his readers, (Revelation 1:4-6).[69] We see the kingdom in the description of the heavenly throne room throughout Revelation 4–5. We see a heavenly choir, God's holy people' (who) sang a song to Jesus including the words, 'You have made them to be a kingdom and...they will reign on the earth' (Revelation 5:10). We see the kingdom also in the fact that a multitude from every nation gathers before God's heavenly throne to praise and worship God on his throne (Revelation 7:9-10). They are joined by worshipping angels, we are told, in verses 11 and 12. There are numerous references to God reigning from his throne throughout Revelation.

In terms of the theology underpinning Revelation Professor Greg Perry is impressed by:

> '...what the book of Revelation teaches us, ... what's happening on the earth is related to what's going on in the heavenlies and that spiritual warfare really has to do with what's really going on in history and what's really going on in our lives.'[70]

Perry brings attention to the connection between what is going on in heaven and what is happening on earth, both in the first century and now. The kingdom is being defined and extended but opposition is being experienced. 'I heard

35

a loud voice in heaven say, "The victory and the power and the kingdom of our God and the authority of his Messiah have now come"' (Revelation 12:10 ERV[71]). The kingdom was being unveiled.

Spiritual conflict

Throughout the book of Revelation John alerted Christians to the spiritual conflict that has been going on since humanity's fall into sin in the Garden of Eden and that will continue until Christ comes again. As the book of Revelation focuses constantly on the king and the kingdom so much is revealed about spiritual warfare to come, such as in chapters 16 and 17, with more detail in the chapters that follow. In chapter 16 we read of God's wrath being poured out against kings and kingdoms at the battle of Armageddon (Revelation 16:16). In chapter 17 there are kingdoms warring against Jesus, the Lamb, but Jesus triumphs '...because he is Lord of lords and King of kings...' (Revelation 17:14). Revelation produces a challenge between God with Christ and his servants on one side and Satan and his servants on the other side. The challenge for us is to take stock and stay firmly on the side of Jesus and his kingdom as we live our lives. This has ever been the challenge for God's people: the Israelites (Jews) of OT days and Christians through the ages. This was the same challenge Joshua as judge put to his people, within their circumstances: '...choose for yourselves this day whom you will serve...as for me and my household, we will serve the Lord' (Joshua 24:15). When there are two destinies, this is the choice![72]

We see in the book of Revelation, near to the end of the first century specifically, and in the world since, that in spiritual circles, warfare has ever been raged between good and evil; between Satan and his servants (evil angels or demons) and God and his servants (faithful angels and Christians). John was exiled because of his uncompromising stand as a Christian during the days of the Roman Empire. In Revelation this empire has fallen. In fact, as we look back over history all the empires that have tried to extinguish the Christian faith have failed. Far from being defeated, God's kingdom has advanced and is continuing to advance to '... every tribe and language and people and nation' (Revelation 5:9; 7:9; 13:7). According to Revelation one day the task will be completed. One of the elders in chapter 7 tells John, 'These are they who have come out of the great tribulation...' (Revelation 7:14a). Then the full number of God's elect will be complete in the victorious kingdom, reigned over by the king.

The new heaven and new earth

Revelation 18 describes the punishment of Babylon, figuratively an evil empire, called in this chapter a prostitute, and the punishment of all the kings and inhabitants of the earth who followed her. Revelation 20 recounts the final defeat of the dragon and his armies and chapters 21 and 22 teach that the new heaven and new earth will be completely free from the presence of evil. The future will be secured; the kingdom will be complete.

Steve Brown, author, broadcaster and professor, sums up this situation:

'When all God's enemies have been rendered powerless, the great spiritual war will end, and God's faithful people will live in uninterrupted peace.'[73]

This will be the ultimate state of God's kingdom and protection. When battles have been fought and won, the king is victorious and the kingdom of God is the only remaining kingdom, we will receive our glorious inheritance in the new heaven and the new earth and be at peace with each other and with our God: Father, Son and Holy Spirit. What a prospect! The first word of this chapter is 'Hallelujah.' May it be the last also: Hallelujah!

3 | Jesus and the values of the kingdom

The restoration of the Kingdom

In the first two chapters surveying Old and New Testaments the present writer has attempted to establish that the kingdom in the OT came to the forefront as a physical kingdom but, in the background, there were veiled references to it being a spiritual kingdom.

In the NT the kingdom refers almost exclusively to the spiritual kingdom and in the background was the physical kingdom. It was not a physical kingdom, however, with the whole country under the authority of a Jewish king. Each region of the Jewish nation had its own king such as '... Herod king of Judea...' (Luke 1:5) who managed his own people as regent of part of the Roman Empire under the Roman governor appointed by Caesar. Herod was king between 4 BC and 39 AD, but politically, the Jewish kings were ineffective puppets under the dominance of the emperor, such as Caesar Augustus (27 BC-14 AD), the emperor at the time of the birth of Jesus (Luke 2:1).

At the trial of Jesus, the emperor was Caesar Tiberius (42 BC-37 AD), and his governor was Pilate. '"...Shall I crucify your king?" Pilate asked. "We have no king but Caesar," the chief priests answered"' [74] (John 19:15). Under the emperor in Rome, Pontius Pilate (20 BC- c36 AD) governed the Jews in Israel; people who were regarded by Rome to be an unruly nation and he therefore had to take on demanding situations such as the trial of Jesus (Matthew 27:2). Judaism was permitted to continue its worship, so the High Priest at the time of the trial of Jesus was Caiaphas (14 BC-46 AD) (in post:18-37 AD) (Matthew 26:57).

One exceptional event three years earlier occurred on a mountainside on the very edge of Israel by the Syrian border. The audience saw and were impressed by the miracles of Jesus and flocked to him in considerable numbers. They were listening to Jesus teaching before and after the 'Feeding of the 5000' miracle. That is why the gospel of John records why the people wanted to make Jesus a king by force (John 6:15), but Jesus would not allow them to do it.

During the ministry of Jesus, there were four scenarios relevant at this point:

The spiritual people were waiting for God to be revealed and bring redemption;

The ordinary people wanted to force the Romans out of their country by having an effective king;

The Roman Governor was trying to keep uprisings down to please the Roman emperor and so keep his position;

The Jewish king was trying to hold the country and fellow Jewish countrymen together and not upset Rome, and so keep *his* position.

This, then, is the background to the disciples' request to Jesus for freedom when '...they...asked him, "Lord, are you at this time going to restore the kingdom to Israel?"' (Acts 1:6). They must have been so frustrated because of being an occupied and oppressed country and continued to be lacking in understanding that Jesus' kingdom was a spiritual and not a physical kingdom. It was virtually impossible for the small Jewish kingdom to be taken from Roman control and established as a free country by military force.

These misunderstandings persisted during the ministry of Jesus. Although the Jewish nation as an occupied country wanted to be released from the Romans and set free, the Romans would never allow it. They were highly disciplined and highly organised. However, we must see the freedom and restoration Jesus *could* bring in an example of how he could reveal the kingdom of which he was (and still is) king. For this we will investigate John's gospel and a particular example of this and see the deity of Christ revealed in healing power and Jesus' amazing application and the salvation he brings, thus displaying and spreading his kingdom. The kingdom is not mentioned by name but we see it in compassion and in action.

John 5 introduces us to a disabled (paralysed) man at the Pool of Bethesda. The man's daily visit to the pool must have seemed like a life-sentence. It had gone on for nearly four decades with no change; no healing. But he lived in hope. His condition was serious, and his future was uncertain.

The healing at the pool

(*Some ancient documents do not have the words in Italics;* For effect, the words of Jesus are **emphasised**). We read in John 5:

'Some time later, Jesus went up to Jerusalem for one of the Jewish festivals. Now there is in Jerusalem near the Sheep Gate a pool, which in Aramaic is called Bethesda and which is surrounded by five covered colonnades. Here a great number of disabled people used to lie—the blind, the lame, the paralysed – *'and they waited for the moving of the waters' (v3b). 'From time to time an angel of the Lord would come down and stir up the waters. The first one into the pool after each such disturbance would be cured of whatever disease they had' (v4).*[75] One who was there had been an invalid for thirty-eight years. When Jesus saw him lying there and learned that he had been in this condition for a long time, he asked him, **"Do you want to get well?"**

"Sir," the invalid replied, "I have no one to help me into the pool when the water is stirred. While I am trying to get in, someone else goes down ahead of me."

Then Jesus said to him, **"Get up! Pick up your mat and walk."** At once the man was cured; he picked up his mat and walked.

The day on which this took place was a Sabbath, and so the Jewish leaders said to the man who had been healed, "It is the Sabbath; the law forbids you to carry your mat."

But he replied, "The man who made me well said to me, **'Pick up your mat and walk.'"**

So they asked him, "Who is this fellow who told you to pick it up and walk?"

The man who was healed had no idea who it was, for Jesus had slipped away into the crowd that was there.

Later Jesus found him at the temple and said to him, **"See, you are well again. Stop sinning or something worse may happen to you."** The man went away and told the Jewish leaders that it was Jesus who had made him well.

(John 5:1-15).

The authority of the Son

So, because Jesus was doing these things on the Sabbath, the Jewish leaders began to persecute him. In his defence Jesus said to them, **"My Father is always at his work to this very day, and I too am working."** For this reason, they tried all the more to kill him; not only was he breaking the Sabbath, but he was even calling God his own Father, making himself equal with God.'

(John 15:16-18)

There are particular things in this passage we must give special attention to:

Special water?

I have lived near Tunbridge Wells, Kent, and have visited Matlock in Derbyshire and Bath in Somerset. All three places have spring water which people have 'taken' (drunk) for centuries[76] believing it has healing properties. A number of these towns have thermal or medicinal springs or both, rising from deep underground. I have not made journeys to 'take the waters' but years ago many people did and travelled great distances across the UK to enjoy their properties including hydrotherapy. The water coming to the surface with its particular smell, temperature and chemicals is special and can still be bought at source.

The Pool of Bethesda, at the time of Jesus near the Lion's Gate, also known as Sheep Gate or St Stephen's Gate, in Jerusalem, was built in the C8th BC to bring rainwater from a reservoir into the city because there was a shortage of water there. The Bible does not claim for it to have thermal or medicinal properties but the link with the angelic visit and healing appears to be authentic Scripture and the reason Jesus visited the Pool and performed the important miracle being studied here. This displays his power over disease and to show his kingdom in his teaching and in restorative action. In his sovereignty he knew the man in desperate need would be there before he arrived.

The paralysed man

At the pool the paralysed man thought he knew that the answer to his problem was found in getting into the Pool of Bethesda as the first person at the visitation of the angel. But for him this did not happen, although he had seen it happen for others. Unexpectedly on one day he finds out that the answer to his problem of needing healing was when Jesus intervened in his life. Jesus asked him a surprising question: 'Do you want to get well?' Of course he did! That was the only reason he was there and he had been waiting to be first into the *disturbed* water for 38 years! This question was to cause the man to have to vocalise his inner need and served as a challenge to his faith. (This was the approach Jesus often took with individuals to draw out of them their longing and faith). The man did not ask to be healed but just described his physical unsurmountable problem preventing healing in that he had no one to put him in the water when the strange phenomenon of the angelic visit occurred occasionally and stirred up the water. Jesus had a dramatic effect on the man's life by restoring his body to wholeness. Word of this healing and its circumstances, on what happened to be the Sabbath, quickly spread to the Jewish leaders, probably the Pharisees. They hated what they heard and despised Jesus for it. The man got up, lifted his mat, and walked away. What a wonderful result! What a wonderful day!

The man's friends

The disabled man was paralysed and so would not have been able to get to the pool on his own and could not get into the pool when he was there without help. No one was able or prepared to help him. We can therefore assume that the man had friends who took him to the pool every day and left him there and they went on their way. The man was then all alone. Sadly, when the angel visited and excitement amongst those there rose, he could not get into the water. I imagine the friends would have had quite a shock when they went to pick him up (literally) that night and were told by disabled people at the pool they were not needed because the man could now walk and had left for the temple! But we must give them credit for transporting the man to and from the pool for 38 years! Something motivated them to do this.

The Jewish leaders

The leaders, who were in all probability constantly following and looking for faults in Jesus, immediately find and complain to the healed man that because he is walking around carrying his mat he was working and therefore breaking the Sabbath laws. This was their major problem with the incident. That misuse of the Sabbath day, in their opinion, was more important to them than the healing. They were legalistic, not compassionate. The man said he was following the instructions of Jesus, so the religious leaders therefore went out of their way to find Jesus and 'persecute him' (John 5:16) for breaking their Sabbath laws. The very least is that they would harass Jesus and try and show him up in public. He explains to them that God is his Father and as God is at work every day so he, Jesus, must be working as well. This made them so angry they wanted to kill Jesus because they could see he was '...calling God his own Father, making himself equal with God' (John 5:18).

Jesus

It is interesting that Jesus is in Jerusalem for a festival, but we are not told why he is at the pool. What we do know is that, in their culture, the pool was a place Jews felt was a disgrace because it was a place where there were people with obvious disabilities. In their prejudice against disability, they disliked that. Jesus counteracts this and changes it by his actions from a place of *disgrace* to a place of *grace*. As with the meaning of its name: Bethesda ('House of Mercy' in Hebrew), it is the place where the man receives mercy and the grace of God.

Jesus concentrates on one individual and on the man's restoration and renewal. In this incident he finds the man twice: first time at the pool, second time at the temple. First time to deal with the man's physical need. Second time to deal with the man's spiritual need. First time in his desperate need of something to happen. Second time when the man was trying to understand what had just happened. This gracious approach took the man forward in his faith. The healed man might even have gone to the temple to praise and thank God for his healing after years of waiting. Before that over an extended period, he might have often been in prayer for healing and for years waited for an answer to his prayers which, for 38 long years, did not come. This could be why Jesus links his healing to his sin. It is possible the paralysis is connected with his lifestyle or with his sin. In making the connection, Jesus was also giving the man the power to overcome the sin he was prone to or which had brought him such suffering and isolation. He, as we all do, have a responsibility to live a life '...worthy of the calling you have received' (Ephesians 4:1), bringing our sin to Jesus for pardon and deliverance on a regular basis.[77]

Jesus does not answer the man's questions about the angel and does not discuss or confirm whether the angel really did visit the pool. That was not the point of the story and carried no importance in the miracle. He was not concerned about upsetting the Jewish leaders or their perception of his law-breaking. He was much more concerned to put things right in the life of one person and move the kingdom of God forward.

The end of the story (John 5:16-18) is an epilogue. Jesus defended his use of the Sabbath and brought attention to God working on the Sabbath and so *he* worked on the Sabbath.[78] We see in the leaders' reactions a deteriorating attitude towards Jesus in the gospels which went from dislike, mainly because he was so popular with the ordinary people, to persecution of Jesus and on to a descent to the depths of trying to kill Jesus.

Despite opposition, Jesus was concerned to reveal the kingdom and teach and display its principles, purpose and power, which he and his cousin, John, announced at the start of their ministries. This went beyond the superficial and superfluous laws of human origin added to God's revealed laws, to an act of kindness and transformation. It was a new way to live. It was the way of renewal, restoration and redemption.

What do we learn?

We see not only that the water is not special, it is not a hot spring and does not contain chemicals or have healing properties. The participants at the pool *are not* claiming that, but they *are* of the opinion, based on experience, that a visit from an angel brings the opportunity for the angel's presence to go against the laws of nature and bring about healing. In other words, the water is disturbed because of the angel's involvement. No angel – no disturbance to the water. No movement of a disabled person trying to be first 'in' – no chance of healing. The stakes were high but the conditions for healing were simple.

There are, of course, details that we do not know. We don't know the number of people who had experienced healing because of being first in. We don't know whether or not this was a tourist attraction and some were making money out of 'residents' or visitors. We don't know why the paralysed man kept coming for almost four decades and how he managed to live without a job or financial support or if he did have income, where it came from. We can only guess at answers to these questions.

We do not know how the friends of the man organised themselves. Did they have a rota? Did they ever try and dissuade the man from attending a failed situation, at least for the man? I wonder if the friends were embarrassed with their task, and I wonder what they thought when the man was healed – the equivalent of winning the lottery!

The Jewish leaders had a great dislike for Jesus. They were unable to do miracles. They could not get people to follow them, as happened naturally with Jesus with his amazing teaching, miracles and acts of great love and kindness with humility. They tried so hard to please God and put on 'a good show' for the ordinary people who admired their evident religiousness and piety. Yet, they did not have the assurance of eternal life, forgiveness of sin and hope for the future that the simplest ordinary Jew had who trusted Jesus as Saviour. The leaders were filled with jealousy and envy and as we read the gospels, they are often meeting and discussing how to deal with Jesus. In the end, of course, they found a way. A cruel way.

Jesus was so patient and merciful to a man with simple needs looking for a solution but looking in the wrong direction. At both meetings with him Jesus gave the man something special.

I have heard it said, 'How do you spell love?' The answer is T-I-M-E![79] Yes, Jesus gave the man time. This whole story with its fascinating few details and absence of other details just confirms who Jesus is and what his mission truly was. I feel sure the man's life would have dramatically changed forever. Jesus gave him the power to overcome sin in his words of authority and command. He would still be a sinner but would have the means to take his sin to God for forgiveness. He would also now have the means to earn a living and have self-respect at last. Jesus said he came to bring life to the spiritually dead (John 5:21). This he did as he restored and reclaimed the paralysed man, and brought him into his kingdom!

Just before he died, the composer, Phillip Bliss (1838-1876) wrote the following in 1875,

'Man of sorrows what a name,
For the Son of God who came.
Ruined sinners to reclaim:
Hallelujah, what a Saviour!'[80]

Yes, Jesus, the Saviour, proved he was and is the King and his mission to display and extend his kingdom with all its spiritual qualities is seen in this thrilling and challenging story. Indeed, as Bliss says,

'Hallelujah, what a Saviour!'

Jesus and the message of the kingdom

4

Just a few years ago, there were times when my computer did not seem to do what I wanted it to do. I gave it too many instructions and it froze, and when it did I had to switch off, let it sort itself out then switch back on again. I think my present computer must be more sophisticated. It does not freeze! Also, I am a more competent user! I am not sure if it is a 'man thing' or personal to me, but, and my wife would endorse this, if I receive too many instructions, I quickly get to the point of overload and cannot cope so easily or know what to do first. My sorting of priorities gets muddled, and I get frustrated.

Understanding the central message of the ministry of Jesus is like this. We saw in chapter two of this book that Jesus was not going to deliver the Jews from Rome, rather, he was establishing who he was: the king of his spiritual kingdom. His focus was the kingdom of God. Then we saw an example of this in chapter three with the paralysed man. Here was evidence of the kingdom at work involving heal-ing: physical and spiritual. Jesus came to bring restoration and redemption, forgiveness of sin and hope with God for eternity. The gospels in general and this story in particu-lar as our example showed Jesus entered the battleground against Satan for people's souls in personal prayer, daily ministry and on the cross, and came out of the battle victori-ous. As the end of the gospels show, it was only by enduring death on the cross and by resurrection that the battle was won. The message of the kingdom is one of victory over sin achieved through suffering. The evidence for this is clear, sufficient and complete in the NT. My main source of the message of the kingdom in this chapter is found in Matthew, Mark and Luke: the Synoptic gospels.

Matthew

Jesus was born in Bethlehem, went to Egypt with his mother, Mary, and stepfather, Joseph, to protect Jesus as caring parents from Herod's cruel massacre of the babies and young children, then returned but to Nazareth with Mary and Joseph who lived there before Bethlehem. At one point he moved to his own home in Capernaum soon after the start of his ministry (Matthew 4:13) to fulfil prophecy (Isaiah 9:1-2). It was based here that Jesus began his ministry as a rabbi at the age of 30, preaching repentance because of the nearness of the kingdom. We read, 'From that time on Jesus began to preach, "Repent, for the kingdom of heaven has come near"' (Matthew 4:17). The Greek 'has come near' also means 'has drawn near.' Four Corner Ministries, a Global Christian Resource Database operating from Innaloo, Western Australia, in their blog adds,

'It does not quite seem to affirm the full arrival of the kingdom at this point. And indeed, since this is at the beginning of Jesus' ministry rather than after his death and resurrection, even the fully realised eschatological approach would acknowledge that there is more to come... a new era is dawning in human history.'[81]

When Jesus, later in his three-year ministry was being crit-icised as usual by the Pharisees in their private discussions and in their minds and they decide he was acting with authority from Satan (Matthew 12:24), he asked them how Satan could drive out Satan, and if he does, 'How then can his kingdom stand?' (v26) Then, knowing their thoughts he said, '...If it is by the Spirit of God that I drive out demons, then the kingdom of God has come upon you' (v28). This put the Pharisees in a dilemma. What was motivating Jesus? Who was giving him power and authority? Was it Satan or God? They were spiritual and logical enough to know it was one or the other. It is inter-esting that ordinary people, without a political or religious axe to grind, could see more clearly than their biased religious leaders. So, Jesus gave the Pharisees a stern warning that if anyone spoke against him they could potentially be forgiven but if anyone attributed his words and actions to the Holy Spirit and they spoke against the Holy Spirit, then they would never be forgiven, not in the present life, nor in eternity (v32).

The inference from this is that these new supernatural signs and wonders in the casting out of Satan from occu-pying and controlling people's hearts, are a sign that the messianic age is revealed in these events occurring in front of on-lookers. The kingdom is beginning to arrive. But if the messianic age, the age of God's royal reign and kingdom are here, then the Messiah must be here. Jesus is actually saying and showing *I am the Messiah.* I have arrived!

However, the kingdom can be either accepted or rejected. God does not force people into a particular decision and the kingdom, strange as it sounds, can be linked with violence. 'From the days of John the Baptist until now, the kingdom of heaven has been subjected to violence, and violent people have been raiding it' (Matthew 11:12 NIVUK), '...and the violent take it by force' (KJV). John had been imprisoned. In the near future, Jesus would be crucified. Therefore, God's new kingly power on earth generated this visible reaction. The kingdom was present and had arrived in the ministry of Jesus. But not everyone could see it. Not everyone accepted him.

Mark

Mark reports Jesus as saying, '"The time has come," he said. "The kingdom of God has come near. Repent and believe the good news!"' (Mark 1:15; Matthew 12:28) There is a slight difference between these two gospel accounts which is refreshing, encouraging and affirms that these were from two different eyewitnesses[82] and not one borrowed from the other. Hence there are differences and similarities in the accounts. Jesus said the news was 'good' but not everyone saw it that way. A considerable number of people came to Jesus (Mark 1:33); they even searched for him when they could not find him (v36-37). But we do not read of mass conversions. Only a limited number of people seemed to believe in Jesus and followed him or found him, not because of his message but because they wanted healing. One person with faith behind his longing for healing was the man with leprosy (v40). To escape the pressure and people wanting him just for healing, Jesus '...stayed outside in lonely places. Yet the people still came to him from everywhere' (v45).

Luke

We must also consider Luke's account, and note his source material may well be Mary since much of his gospel is from her perspective.[83] We read, 'Once, on being asked by the Pharisees when the kingdom of God would come, Jesus replied, "The coming of the kingdom of God is not something that can be observed, nor will people say, "Here it is" or "There it is," because the kingdom of God is in your midst' (Luke 17:20-21). This is a reminder that the kingdom is not restricted to one person, place, or nation. The kingdom of God is present with people whenever Jesus was present with them and with the presence of Jesus, God's royal reign is present. It had arrived with the ministry of Jesus.

So, what is the message?

The message of the kingdom is clear. God reigns over the established spiritual kingdom in the hearts of those who love Jesus the king. His people enter the kingdom by faith. This is what victory looks like but is achieved through the suffering of Jesus, God's king, as Isaiah makes plain in calling him a '...man of suffering...' (*promising*) '...the will of the Lord will prosper in his hand' (Isaiah 53: 3, 10). (*Emphasis mine*). This was difficult for most Jews to accept, both then in OT days and during the ministry of Jesus. That is why we read of the Jews mistaken intentions and of Jesus' unwillingness to co-operate with them, such as when they tried to make him king by force (John 6:15). The Jews expected a triumphant king without understanding how he would triumph. This is, however, Jesus' kingdom mission and at the end of the age, he is the heavenly king who will come on the clouds to judge the world. However, first he had to die on the cross in his earthly body for the sins of his people and rise from the dead in his heavenly body. This paradoxical reality of a suffering king is a vital theme that we have already considered and will return to.

The kingdom examined

The message of the kingdom is one of redemption. This gives it significant importance which we will examine further by looking at or re-visiting salient points. Contrary to expectations, and the physical kingdom of the OT as well as the Jewish kingdom of the NT under the dominance of Rome, it was not a mighty king who appeared at a coronation but a baby in a manger. Therefore, Mark says in his first chapter, 'The time has come' (NIVUK) or, better as, 'The time is fulfilled' (KJV) (Mark 1:15). Israel had longed for a powerful king. This was also on the minds of the '...Magi... (*who came*) from the east to Jerusalem and asked, "Where is the one who has been born King of the Jews?...' (Matthew 2:1b-2a). (*Emphasis mine*). They (Jews and wise men) looked for a strong man and found a baby! The wise men naturally went to the royal palace in the capital city where they expected the king to be. Herod was truly angry to think he may have a rival and hence he wanted to kill the baby and remove the threat to his position, (Matthew 2:3, v13, v16).[84]

The facts need to be re-examined. Where the king is, that is where the kingdom is. That is why Jesus says to the Pharisees, '...the kingdom of God is in your midst' (Luke 17:21). This is *the place* where the kingdom is. *The purpose* of the kingdom is as found in Luke, where Jesus says he 'must proclaim the good news of the kingdom' (Luke 4:43). The kingdom contains *and is* good news. The news is that sin can be forgiven by faith through grace and people can have peace with God and eternal life in his kingdom with him.

Through his preaching, actions and invitation Jesus presents the kingdom and invites people to enter it. Luke summarises Jesus' ministry as '...the knowledge of the secrets of the kingdom of God' (Luke 8:10), and Jesus demonstrates this in his 60 or so parables. About half are about present and gradual growth and the other half are about a sudden crisis in the future. Jesus often spoke parables that illustrated the *message* of the kingdom. Luke records, 'While a large crowd was gathering and people were coming to Jesus from town after town, he told them this parable...' (Luke 8:4). This was the Parable of the Sower. Jesus also demonstrates the *power* of the kingdom, as in his challenge to the Pharisees when he asks them, 'But If I drive out demons by the finger of God, then the kingdom of God has come upon you (Luke 11:20). This drew out those spiritually searching and put the Pharisees on the 'back foot' with their accusative arguments.

Jesus is training his followers (Luke 10:1-25): the 12 disciples and others for a time when he will not be with them in person. So, he sends them out as ambassadors of the kingdom to herald its arrival. He had already sent out the 12, now he appoints 72 more to be sent out. It was a tough assignment. They went to towns ahead of his visit as 'lambs among wolves' (v3) engaging with 'the enemy' (v19). It was spiritual warfare and this is why Jesus later declared to Pilate at his trial, "...My kingdom is not of this world..." (John 18:36). This warfare would always be on his mind. He looked to his followers as he sent them out to gain the same insight and knowledge by personal experience that he as King and Lord had. A central message they were to share was, 'The kingdom of God has come near' (Luke 10:11). They return after their kingdom preaching with joy, and Jesus is filled with joy (v17, v21), because he '...saw Satan fall like lightening from heaven' (v18). Satan was unsettled and unseated.

Jesus achieves and redeems the kingdom and its citizens fully through his death and resurrection. He defeats Satan and those who rebel against his rule, and he overcame sin and death by giving himself as the perfect sacrifice. As Paul expressed it in writing to the Christians at Colossae with his bold and commanding use of language, he says that Jesus:

> 'having cancelled the charge of our legal indebtedness, which stood against us and condemned us; he has taken it away, nailing it to the cross. And having disarmed the powers and authorities, he made a public spectacle of them, triumphing over them by the cross' (Colossians 2:14-15).

His three-year ministry and the experience of his followers was a precursor of what was to happen at his crucifixion where he overcame the world, the flesh and the Devil by destroying the power of the kingdom of darkness – spiritually speaking. In other words: the kingdom of the world. Jesus proved that at the cross he is the rightful ruler of the restored kingdom.

In wanting the attention of Jesus, his family misunderstood him (Matthew 12:46). At the Transfiguration, the disciples, led by Peter, blurted things out which showed they misunderstood him (Matthew 17:1-9). At his trial Pilate, in asking if he was the king of the Jews, misunderstood him (Luke 23:3). It is, therefore, not surprising that after three years living closely with Jesus, and seeing and hearing his amazing life and teaching his disciples could not comprehend the true nature of his kingdom and misunderstood him (Acts 1:6). Right up to leaving the earth to ascend to his heavenly Father, the disciples asked of him their final question. That concerned the nature of his kingdom and whether or not he was going to overthrow Roman occupation! They still misunderstood him. It was a spiritual kingdom requiring spiritual understanding accepted by faith.[85]

First mention of the kingdom in the Lord's Prayer

We must now consider further teaching by Jesus in the greatest prayer ever prayed. We call it The Lord's Prayer. It is such an important prayer carrying such a vital message of the kingdom it is approached here and covered in other chapters of this book as well.

The Lord's Prayer is a title given to it by Bible translators simply because Jesus gave a perfect framework for his followers to pray at that time and for the future. It could be entitled the Christian's prayer since it is a pattern for Christians to adopt. In terms of computer use we could call it a template. In my teaching career I often attended school staff meetings at which I was chairing and taking the Minutes, if I was short of a secretary to take them for me. I was prepared with a template on my laptop. This enabled me to professionally chair the meeting, concentrate on and listen to what was discussed, and record what was decided under various prepared headings. The Lord's Prayer is a little like this. It fixes for us petition importance and priority and serves as a template for our prayers. Luke has a summary of the prayer (Luke 11:2-4), Matthew's version is fuller in which Jesus said,

'This, then, is how you should pray:

Our Father in heaven,
hallowed be your name,
your kingdom come,
your will be done,
on earth as it is in heaven.
Give us today our daily bread.
and forgive us our debts,
as we also have forgiven our debtors.
And lead us not into temptation,
but deliver us from the evil one.
For yours is the kingdom
and the power and the glory forever.
Amen'
(Matthew 6:9-13).[86]

Jesus tells us to pray, 'Your kingdom come...' (Matthew 6:10), but what does this mean? What are we praying for when we make this petition? There is a logic that runs like a thread through the Lord's Prayer. A sort of priority list of petitions. Each of the petitions is linked to the others. The first petition Jesus taught is, '...hallowed be your name,' (v9) which is a plea that the name of God would be reverenced as holy. It is the first step. Unless this is so, his kingdom will not and cannot come into this world. So, we who regard his name as holy have the responsibility to openly declare the kingdom of God in and by our lives and in and by our words. These are the profoundly serious words of Jesus. They are a command.

Heaven is God's kingdom and he is sovereign in it. It is his realm over which he reigns. There is no sin there and he has no rival there. Any revolt was decisively crushed and evil angels expelled from heaven a long time ago (2 Peter 2:4; Jude v6). As R.T. Kendall (b.1935), preacher and writer, says there is only worship there,

> '...by all the angelic creation as well as all the believers who have died.'[87]

Kendall goes on to explain that God's kingdom extends to earth as well. One day believers will reign with him over everything, but not yet (Hebrews 2:8). This is why we pray 'Your kingdom come.' This will happen at the Second Coming of Jesus with power and glory and the total defeat of evil through '...his appearing and his kingdom...' (2 Timothy 4:1). 'Then the end will come, when he hands over the kingdom to God the Father after he has destroyed all dominion, authority and power.' (1 Corinthians 15:24). We must remember that the kingdom is not just future, it is also present tense. This is how we understand the kingdom to be established and yet we pray for it to come. We pray for the kingdom to come in our witness with the gospel and at the point when believers enter it and pray for it to come in completion at the Second Coming of Jesus.

Second mention of the kingdom in the Lord's Prayer

At the end of The Lord's Prayer, we again pray the truth that to God belongs '...the kingdom, and the power and the glory...' (Matthew 6:13). In this, we honour and reverence God and our own inheritance of the kingdom by God's grace. It is God's pleasure to give it to us but at the right time and in his chosen way. Jesus commands us, '...seek his kingdom...

Do not be afraid little flock, for your Father has been pleased to give you the kingdom' (Luke 12:31a, v32).

This is why the message continues to be proclaimed and is the restoration and redemption in the kingdom gradually being unveiled at the present and which will continue into the future.

The spiritual Kingdom

5

As the spiritual kingdom of God is a recurring theme through both testaments of the Bible we need to understand the meaning behind this phrase. It is a spiritual kingdom but we need to be clear what we mean by this.

I am aware that there are diverse ways of expressing the kingdom. Jesus assured his hearers that God the Father knew Christians needed practical basic things and added, 'But seek first his kingdom and righteousness, and all these things will be given to you as well' (Matthew 6:33). From the coming of Jesus to begin the kingdom we see a clear picture of the Gospel. The kingdom is outlined in several different ways in the NT:

> *Matthew* has 'kingdom' (Matthew 6:13); 'his kingdom' (13:41); 'your kingdom' (6:10, 20:21); and 'the kingdom of heaven' (3:2; 4:17; 13:11; 13:24).
> *Mark* uses the phrase 'the coming kingdom of our father' (Mark 11:10)[88]; and 'kingdom of God' (Mark 1:14-15).
> *Luke* also has 'kingdom of God' (Luke 4:43).
> *Paul* to the Christians in Ephesus has 'the kingdom of Christ and of God' [Ephesians 5:5].

Even though the exact wording differs between Christ, God and heaven, these and other examples are symbols of the same concept but with different emphases.

In summary, according to the editor of Christianity.com, there are three things that the Kingdom of God means:

1. 'The rule of Jesus Christ on earth;
2. The blessing and privileges that flow from living under Christ's rule;
3. The citizens of this kingdom, the Church, are within it.'[89]

How important is the spiritual kingdom?

We can understand the importance of the spiritual kingdom of God by examining the gospels. In Matthew we see the highest priority of John the Baptist and Jesus who call for repentance because 'the kingdom of God has come near' (3:2; 4:17). When Jesus is teaching the disciples how to pray, we see just the word 'kingdom' is a central feature (6:10, 13). In the Beatitudes Jesus used the phrase 'kingdom of heaven' and said it was belonging to 'the poor in spirit' (5:3) and to 'those who are persecuted' (5:10). He also speaks of the 'gospel of the kingdom' (24:14). Matthew uses the phrase 'kingdom of heaven' when announcing the rule or reign of Jesus because he is being sensitive to his Jewish countrymen who in religious strictness would not use the sacred name of God. Jesus encouraged people to 'seek first' his kingdom. This is his highest spiritual priority.

At the Last Supper, as throughout his ministry, the kingdom was on Jesus' mind as he said, 'Truly I tell you, I will not drink again from the fruit of the vine until that day when I drink it new in the kingdom of God' (Mark 14:25).

The facts of the spiritual kingdom

God's rule

James Hamilton, professor of Biblical theology and Baptist pastor, Kentucky, writes in his Blog: Knowing God: Kingdom:

> 'Any kingdom will consist of a king, his realm, its citizens, and the law that regulates their lives. This is true of God's kingdom as well. We must briefly see the Bible's presentation of God's rule over God's people in God's place according to God's law.'[90]

Even though we know of God's kingdom it is hard to keep it at the forefront of our hearts and minds. This is because it is such a mysterious concept. It is dynamic in nature and refers primarily to the rule of the king. As seen in the OT, the kingdom was used in a physical sense to refer to a nation and territory. As a result, in the vast majority of instances, it would be better to consider the expression 'kingdom of God' as meaning the 'rule of God,' as suggested in Baker's Evangelical Dictionary, a Christian reference work.[91]

God's kingdom is established

Since God is the Creator of everything, he reigns over everything. His role as Creator establishes his authority over the earth and all of his creation. His kingdom is universal (1 Timothy 6:15). At the same time the kingdom of God involves repentance and the new birth as God rules in the hearts of his children in this world in preparation for the next. The work begun on earth will find its consummation in heaven (Philippians 1:6). We read of the kingdom being secure:

> 'The earth is the Lord's, and everything in it, the world, and all who live in it.'
> (Psalm 24:1)

'The Lord has established his throne in heaven, and his kingdom rules over all.' (Psalm 103:19)
'For in him all things were created: things in heaven and on earth, visible and invisible, whether thrones or powers or rulers or authorities; all things have been created through him and for him. He is before all things, and in him all things hold together.' (Colossians 1:16-17)

God created people and gave them authority and control over the earth. In creating the universe, he designed it and established his kingdom on his terms and wanted people to be citizens of it. This was his plan and it centred around the opportunity for people to participate with him to enter it and live with him forever.

God's heavenly kingdom and earthly kingdom are opposed by Satan

The Bible speaks of rebellion against God by Satan and his evil angels. This led to their fall and eviction from heaven. Satan then established his own kingdom on earth to defy God. This is summarised as follows:

'How you have fallen from heaven, morning star, son of the dawn! You have been cast down to the earth, you who once laid low the nations!' (Isaiah 14:12)
'...The dragon stood in front of the woman who was about to give birth, so that it might devour her child the moment he was born' (Revelation 12:4b).9[2]
'The god of this age has blinded the minds of unbelievers, so that they cannot see the light of the gospel

that displays the glory of Christ, who is the image of God' (2 Corinthians 4:4).

Satan was ejected from heaven and he continues to oppose God from his own kingdom on earth. When Jesus was born Satan was angry and tried through the life and death of Jesus to retaliate against God. He still continues to work tirelessly on the earth, in his kingdom. He works for his own glory and for his own benefit and makes life difficult for everyone and is especially against Christians and he constantly opposes the spreading of the gospel. He never gives up. This is why Peter advises Christians, 'Be alert and of sober mind. Your enemy the devil prowls around like a roaring lion looking for someone to devour' (1 Peter 5:8).

God's kingdom is re-established

Though sin has been inherited by humanity, God chose and called out a people for himself to worship him and be his own special family. The human family began with Adam. Israel, the particular nation family of God's choice, came from Abraham. Through a covenant with Abraham, God promised he would re-establish his kingdom and authority on earth and give his family special blessing. He said, 'I will make you a great nation, and I will bless you; I will make your name great, and you will be a blessing....and all peoples on earth will be blessed through you' (Genesis 12:2, v3b). He went on to say, 'The whole land of Canaan, where you now reside as a foreigner, I will give as an everlasting possession to you and your descendants after you, and I will be their God' (Genesis 17:8). God promised the growth of the nation, 'I will make your descendants as numerous as the stars in the sky and will give them all these lands, and through your offspring all nations on earth will be blessed' (Genesis 26:4). The result of these wonderful promises is that the Jews would have three things: a land, a nation and a blessing. God's kingdom would advance through this nation family if they acknowledged that they were chosen and set apart for God.

God's kingdom and holiness

Israel went into Egypt to escape the ravishes of famine in Canaan and eventually came out again and went back to their own land. On the way to their land God revealed his will and laws at Sinai and details of his covenant, or agreement, with his people. This meant the people were truly set apart from all other nations on earth. Moses became the reluctant leader and was told by God to tell the people that his name is '...I am who I am. This is what you are to say to the Israelites, "I am has sent me to you"' (Exodus 3:14). The people were to exercise faith and live by their faith and offer sacrifices from a pure heart to receive forgiveness for sin. The sacrifices pointed to the final one of all, that of Jesus who was to give his life as the final and complete sacrifice. That was to be their way of life. The priests were to lead worship and mediate for them with God, and his kingdom citizens must maintain holiness.

These instructions and way of living are summarised in Exodus,

'Then Moses went up to God, and the Lord called to him from the mountain and said, "This is what you are to say to the descendants of Jacob and what you are to tell the people of Israel: You yourselves have seen what I did to Egypt, and how I carried you on eagles' wings and brought you to myself. Now if you obey me fully and keep my covenant, then out of all nations you will be my treasured possession. Although the whole earth is mine, you will be for me a kingdom of priests and a holy nation. These are the words you are to speak to the Israelites"' (Exodus 19:3-6).

God's kingdom comes simply but at the right time

The archangel Gabriel firstly visited Zechariah and told him his barren wife Elizabeth would have a baby who would be the forerunner of the Saviour to come (Luke 1:13, v16). Secondly, Gabriel visited Mary, who was a virgin, to say she would become the mother of '...the Son of God' (Luke 1:35b). God the Holy Spirit would 'overshadow' Mary and so God would be the child's father (Luke 1:35). It would not be Joseph. In this not only is prophecy being fulfilled but God is using chosen people for his special task of re-establishing his kingdom in the right place at the right time. Elizabeth and Mary were related and so John and Jesus were related and ministered alongside each other in spreading the kingdom of God. As covered earlier in this book, John's primary task through his preaching and baptising was to prepare the way for the ministry of Jesus.

God's kingdom is entered by grace through faith

Jesus teaches that we must receive the kingdom of God like a small child (Mark 10:13-16). He uses a child to illustrate dependency by which we are to rely on Christ for our entrance into the kingdom. There must be not only correct actions but also correct attitudes. This teaching indicates that the kingdom is not achieved by our own efforts but obtained by humbly accepting and relying on God as a child relies on a parent. Paul reminds the Christians in Ephesus, 'For it is by grace you have been saved, through faith – and this is not from yourselves, it is the gift of God – not by works, so that no one can boast' (Ephesians 2:8-9). And Paul tells the Christians at Philippi to emulate Christ who always obeyed God, 'Have the same mindset as Christ Jesus' (*who*) 'made himself nothing' (*but*) 'he humbled himself by becoming obedient to death – even death on a cross!' (Philippians 2:7-8) (*Insertions mine*).

Both John the Baptist and Jesus preached repentance as a necessary sign of belonging to the kingdom of God. Too often I see repentance omitted when people are being encouraged to follow Christ but this was not so with John and Jesus. As John expressed it, 'Repent, for the kingdom of heaven has come near' (Matthew 3:2), and Jesus: '...Repent and believe the good news!'" (Mark 1:15) Repentance and belief in Christ really are necessary criteria for birth into the spiritual kingdom. John in his gospel is specific in speaking of new birth by water and the spirit, '...no one can enter the kingdom of God unless they are born of water and the Spirit' (John 3:5). By taking this route as an act of obedience to God's commands, a person enters the spiritual kingdom and the spiritual kingdom enters the person.

God's kingdom is mysterious

Not everything is crystal clear to us but Jesus teaches about the mysteries of the kingdom of God throughout the gospels. Matthew 13 is a chapter of preaching just on the kingdom through parables: the Sower, the Weeds, the Mustard Seed, the Yeast, the Hidden Treasure, the Pearl and the Net. Certain parables are explained in great detail others are left to the hearers to think through. The teaching was so new to the listeners and so dynamic at Nazareth that they admitted, reluctantly on this occasion, that Jesus had great wisdom and miraculous power. Sadly, because they knew his background and family members, they were deeply offended by the content of the parables (v53-57). Their lack of faith led to few miracles in his hometown. His audience had failed to understand the OT and so rejected the kingdom he was introducing with its requirements of repentance and faith to enter.

The challenges of the spiritual kingdom

In my work with children and young people with learning disabilities tasks given to achieve were often met with the response, 'Sir, this is not easy!' or, 'Sir, this isn't fair!' This is so with the challenges of the spiritual kingdom. We would like to have things more our own way or have things required of us that are more understandable and simpler to achieve. But we must do things God's way. We must live as God expects. We must go as God directs.

As we seek the Kingdom of God and as we pray, we are also acknowledging the rule and reign of the kingdom of God in our lives. This is when Jesus is our Saviour and Lord. This was the situation when on one occasion Jesus said the kingdom of God is 'in your midst' (NIVUK) or 'within you' (KJV) (Luke 17:21b), where he was speaking of himself. With Jesus as Lord of one's life, and when he is in control, this is the kingdom of God at work. If this is so, we are in the kingdom of God right now. It is not being religious with rules and regulations, '...but righteousness, and peace, and joy in the Holy Spirit' (Romans 14:17).

In praying the Lord's Prayer and applying it to our lives (Matthew 6:9-13), we pray, 'Your kingdom come, your will be done, on earth as it is in heaven' (v10). The prayer is asking for our own lives to change with Jesus in control and for the kingdom to come as well as the gospel to be spread throughout the earth. We have become a part of God's kingdom when we accept Jesus by faith through grace and we are then called to be witnesses for him in the world. As outlined by Prof. David P. Seemuth, Founder and President of the Centre for Christian Study, Wisconsin, who writes:

'This is our command and commission: to know him and make him known.'[93]

6 Citizenship of the kingdom

In terms of manufacturing on the global stage we live in strange days. When we buy goods an increasing number of them appear to have obsolescence built in. What I mean by this is that if you buy a mobile phone, for instance, the battery lasts just two years before failing, but all the time in use you notice it getting weaker. What I also notice is that my phone contract is for two years and then must be renewed. So, as the battery fails so the phone contract needs renewing. Is this a coincidence? That way I have to take out a new contract invariably at a higher price and so the supplier makes more money out of me. I have found this also happens with other goods. With cars most people accept that on average a car is designed to last for seven years. Few go on beyond that. (Mine is therefore an exception and is in its second life cycle!). Car parts, 'white' goods, electronic devices all have the obsolescence trait.

Thankfully, this is not the case with anything God is involved with! He has designed and established an enduring kingdom. Daniel foretold, it '...will never be destroyed...' (Daniel 2:44). What makes the kingdom so special? It is a kingdom like no other. It has a King like no other. It is absolutely essential to become a citizen of it. We must now move on in our studies to examine what is meant by becoming and being a citizen of the spiritual kingdom of God and what the kingdom became after the death, resurrection and ascension of Jesus who then returned to his Father in heaven. As he is King of the Kingdom, we need to be clear where God reigns.

The Lord reigns

To say that the Lord reigns as King means he reigns as king in the lives of people who love him. So, we are under the new covenant of God's reign in his kingdom; his church. Jesus promised to build his church. Then after he had said this, he promised to give Peter the keys of the kingdom (Matthew 16:18,19). In my experience in education if after an interview a Chair of Governors said you are appointed as Head of this school, here are the keys, it would not make sense if the keys were those of another school. Equally it would not make sense to have the post of running a school and not be trusted with keys to the school to do the job. Peter was given the keys to the kingdom: the church. Here in the church is the realm in which the Lord reigns as King. As already discovered, if we are in Christ, we are in his kingdom. Conversely, we can only say we are in his kingdom, if we are in Christ, (Colossians 1:13).

Citizenship of the United Kingdom

Supposing someone wanted to become a British Citizen, what needs to happen? In an advertisement, a firm of solicitors, seeking customers, begins their advertisement as follows:

'Becoming a British Citizen

There are different ways to become a British citizen, but the most common is called naturalisation. To be naturalised, you need to meet several requirements, including living in the UK for five years or more and intending to continue living here. You must also pass two tests: Knowledge of English and Life in the UK.'[94]

This is followed by citizenship admission details and advice how to proceed. The solicitors advise 'at a price,' and an application for citizenship comes with requirements and also at a price. Nothing is free!

Citizenship of God's kingdom

All nations, including kingdoms, have citizens and they all require immigration status. The kingdom of God is no different. Every kingdom citizen today is a naturalised citizen, brought into the kingdom by the route of new birth. 'For he has rescued us from the dominion of darkness and brought us into the kingdom of the Son he loves' (Colossians 1:13).

We enter the kingdom of heaven through being 'born again.' As we do so, our rebellious former nature is changed into trust in Christ and we receive quite freely forgiveness for our sins and eternal life in our new nature. Having received Christ as Saviour through our new birth, we go on to learn to serve him and allow him to be Lord of our lives. This will be developed in a later chapter (See: Kingdom Citizens, a website where this is further explained).[95]

If the kingdom is the church and the church is a family, what are the implications of saying this? Here we must listen to Paul who wrote a letter to Timothy so that he and the Christians with him '...will know how...to conduct themselves in God's household, which is the church of the living God, the pillar and foundation of the truth' (1 Timothy 3:15). God has a family: that is the church. The head of the church family is God. This means God's family and his kingdom are the same, and God adds saved, born-again people to this church family. We read of the Early Church, '...the Lord added to their number daily those who were being saved' (Acts 2:47b).

When I was a young person and new Christian, I heard Billy Graham preaching in my home city in the North of England. I remember him saying in one part of his sermon, 'How do you become a Christian?' He paused and added, 'It's not by birth.' To reinforce his argument, he further said, 'If you were born in a garage, would that make you a car? No! Being born in England, or being born into your family, or being a regular attender at your church, won't make you a Christian either.' He had the most piercing steely eyes (quite appropriate for a steel-making city) and he seemed to look at individuals as he said, '...You must be born again!' (John 3:7b).

Billy Graham used words from a conversation Jesus had with Nicodemus. He was a Pharisee and a high-status member of the ruling council of Israel, the Sanhedrin. Jesus did not waste words but told Nicodemus, '...no one can enter the kingdom of God unless they are born of water and the Spirit' (John 3:5). So, to be part of the kingdom involves coming to birth twice. Yes, twice!

Body, soul, and spirit

As Jesus said to Nicodemus, there is a way to become a citizen of God's kingdom which, unlike the citizenship of the UK route, does not require passing tests but it does require a response to God, repentance, faith and experience. It is free and by grace. In quite simple terms, the water indicates being born into the world (John 3:5) as a human being with a body, a soul and a spirit (1 Thessalonians 5:23).[96] We know at death the body is laid down and we require it no more. No matter how we try and hang on to it, we have to leave it. It is not designed to go on into eternity. The soul is different. That is our relationship with people and our world around us and it does go on in eternal life to heaven, as Jesus clearly explained, '...whoever has the Son has life...eternal life' (1 John 5:12a, v13b). He also said that the unrepentant and unforgiven soul will be punished, '...be afraid of the One who can destroy both soul and body in hell' (Matthew 10:28b). In the Bible soul is sometimes interchanged with spirit and sometimes separate from the spirit. However, the easiest and clearest way to understand spirit is for us to realise it can come alive when prompted by God the Holy Spirit and this part of us, our spirit, can be 'born again,' as Jesus said to Nicodemus.

As long ago as about a thousand years BC, the writer of Ecclesiastes[97] tells us that after life on earth, '...then people go to their eternal home...and the spirit returns to God who gave it' (Ecclesiastes 12:5b, v7b).

Blessings of the spiritual kingdom

As citizens in the kingdom, those who have been born into God's family have wonderful privileges. These are better described as spiritual blessings. Paul says to the Christians at Ephesus, '...God...has blessed us in the heavenly realms with every spiritual blessing in Christ' (Ephesians 1:3). We are '... children of God through faith' [Galatians 3:26]. There are no distinctions of Jew or Gentile, slave or free, male or female, '...for you are all one in Christ Jesus' (Galatians 3:28). We can call God our 'Father...and since you are his child, God has made you also an heir' (Galatians 4:6-7). We can approach God directly and come freely and present our prayers and requests to him, (Philippians 4:6). In and through Jesus we are accepted and, '...we have redemption, the forgiveness of sins' (Colossians 1:14).

As citizens in the kingdom, we can ask for forgiveness and he will '...forgive us our sins...' (1 John 1:9). We are now able '...to be a holy priesthood, offering spiritual sacrifices acceptable to God through Jesus Christ' (1 Peter 2:5).

As citizens in God's kingdom, we are '...called, chosen and faithful followers' *of Christ.* (Revelation 17:14) (*Insertion mine*). We are in a family with brothers and sisters and so are instructed to '...love each other deeply...' (1 Peter 4:8). We are instructed to be hospitable to one another, serving one another, encouraging one another, forgiving one another, and be praying for one another. (1 Peter 4:9; Galatians 5:13; Colossians 3:13; Hebrews 3:13, James 5:16)

As citizens in God's kingdom, we have an optimistic outlook about the future. We are God's children and as Paul said to the Christians in Galatia, he now says to those in Rome, that we are '...heirs of God and co-heirs with Christ...' (Romans 8:17). Continuing to think of the kingdom, we refer to James who says we '...inherit the kingdom he promised those who love him' (James 2:5). This aptly rounds off the blessings!

History: His story

If History really is His story, (as mentioned in the Introduction to this book), then I am quite insignificant and yet God does not see me that way. To him I am special and am chosen to love him and serve him in his kingdom. He gives to me a new heart and mind. Success and popularity in the world do not compare with the values of the kingdom which are so much higher and purer, and unlike earthly achievements which vanish at death, the values of the kingdom last into eternity. Instead of serving myself in my old nature, my goals have changed. I now want to serve my sovereign God because of all I have come to realise he has done for me, especially in the person of Jesus and his saving work on the cross.

I find as a new creation and citizen of the kingdom that I am more secure than I ever was before I entered the kingdom. I see how God has worked throughout time to guard and keep the world and everything of value to him in it, to redeem his people and cause people, including me, to be in the right place at the right time for circumstances to come together that he might work a lasting work in and through me. In his sovereignty and by his grace, I have come to experience his loving and just character and see the out-working of his plan of salvation for me.

The hymn-writer Arthur Ainger (1841-1919) expressed God's sovereignty in a hymn in 1894:

'God is working his purpose out
as year succeeds to year:
God is working his purpose out,
and the time is drawing near;
nearer and nearer draws the time,
the time that shall surely be,
when the earth shall be filled
with the glory of God
as the waters cover the sea.'[98]

Citizenship of the kingdom also gives a sense of urgency to tell others about Christ and introduce them to the kingdom. As Courtney Whiting from Dallas, Texas, says in her on-line blog,

'God's patience with us will not last forever and at some point, Christ will return. His second coming will not be to redeem, but to judge. Because we do not know the day or time, we are to use our time wisely to help others receive the kingdom through faith in Christ.'[99]

7 The importance of the kingdom

Life can be so remarkably busy. It is therefore important to prioritise what order to do things and to concentrate on those of highest priority. As a junior officer, Custer (1839-1876), who was a cavalry officer from Ohio, became a distinguished soldier in the American Civil War (1861-65), and this earned him promotion. By 1876 at the Battle of Little Bighorn, Custer, now Colonel, was leading the seventh cavalry of the United States Union Army against the Plains Indians. The Native North Americans were regarded as being troublesome, but then they had a long history and resented their freedom being curtailed as land was taken off them. The Sioux and Cheyenne forces of about 2000 men were led by their Chief, Sitting Bull. Custer was outnumbered but fought bravely with his 600 men dividing his troops into three detachments. He died, aged 36, of gunshot wounds to his head and heart having held his hill where he found himself with just 40 men. The battle is now known as 'Custer's Last Stand'. He knew the odds were against him and he was not going to survive this battle. He therefore decided which 'hill to die on.' It was important to him to make his stand and fight for his nation. The bravery of Custer is beyond question.

In 1831 at the cholera outbreak in London Arthur Wellesley, Duke of Wellington (1769-1852), soldier, political leader and twice prime minister, who defeated Napoleon at the Battle of Waterloo in 1815, said,

'The only thing I am afraid of is fear.'100

To Wellington, cholera was important but more important to be feared was fear itself and that was highest in importance and the central priority in his thinking.

The kingdom of God has been won by a vital battle, and Jesus taking a stand against Satan on the cross where he died to achieve victory. Fear did not feature in the stand Jesus took and the establishment of the kingdom was a central and vitally important theme in his preaching. John Piper (b1946), theologian, pastor and chancellor of Bethlehem College and Seminary, Minneapolis, Minnesota, tells us,

> 'In the ESV translation,101 'kingdom' is mentioned 126 times in the Gospels. But then 'kingdom' is mentioned only 34 times in the rest of the New Testament.'102

To add to Piper's summary, 'kingdom' is actually mentioned 55 times in Matthew alone. This encourages me to consider again the crucial question: Why does the kingdom of God get so much prominent, explicit attention in the teaching and preaching of Jesus and far less attention in the rest of the NT? Does this mean that to Jesus it was his highest priority but not so to the non-gospel books of the NT?

In every respect the kingdom is important in relation to what it is and what it does. Several aspects require special attention.

Rule and reign

The kingdom creates a realm and creates a people, but the kingdom of God is not just its realm or just its people. For his own pleasure (and actually for theirs and ours), God created his kingdom and a people to populate it and love him as he loved them. God decided that his king would be revealed through the crucifixion and resurrection, to suffer and die as human and to rise triumphantly in divine glory. As shepherd boy and later as king with time to meditate on God and his creation, David wrote beautiful words we encountered in researching the Spiritual Kingdom chapter. He wrote, 'The Lord has established his throne in heaven, and his kingdom rules over all' (Psalm 103:19). God's rule and reign governs all things from his throne. In his rule, his reign, and his lordship, he is sovereign. As John proclaimed in Revelation (and I like the KJV on this): '...for the Lord God omnipotent reigneth.' For 'omnipotent,' the NIVUK has 'Almighty' (Revelation 19:6).

Redemption and restoration

We have seen that the kingdom has been established, spoiled and re-established. God's purpose is to save and gather a family to himself. This involved redemption and restoration on their behalf. This is why Jesus began his ministry by announcing the kingdom as 'good news' (Luke 4:18). Using the words of Isaiah, John the Baptist heralded the coming of the Messiah and kingdom, (Luke 3:6 using Isaiah 40:3-5). This brought in the new covenant or agreement with God to enter the hearts of his people by triumphing over sin, death and Satan. It also achieved the exercise of his reign gathering saved people to live as citizens of the kingdom. Then, as Courtney Whiting indicated (as in chapter six), the final stage is for Christ to return a second time to the earth but this time in glory and splendour to complete all of God's plans.[103]

Kingdom present; kingdom future

Jesus is present as human (and yet divine) in the Gospels, but not in the rest of the NT, and the Gospels is where we see his teaching about the kingdom. He is establishing it and living it out. The other writers of the NT books write with the kingdom already established and they 'take it in their stride' and concentrate on its application to daily living. We must note, however, that Jesus stresses a *present* dimension and a *future* dimension to the kingdom. Both aspects, or dimensions, are present in the two mentions of the kingdom in the Lord's Prayer: '...yours is the kingdom...' (*present*) and '...your kingdom come...' (*future*) (Matthew 6:13b, v10a). (*Emphasis mine*) Jesus, in preaching on the kingdom, had to address his hearers' thinking and take them from the physical to the spiritual kingdom. They thought of the kingdom in physical form and '...that the kingdom of God was going to appear at once' (Luke 19:11b). However, Jesus used phrases (recorded in the Gospels) such as:

'...the kingdom of heaven has come near' (Matthew 3:2);

'...receive the kingdom of God like a little child...' (Mark 10:15);

'...the kingdom of God has come upon you' (Luke 11:20b);

'...the kingdom of God is in your midst' (Luke 17:21);

'...no one can see the kingdom of God unless they are born again' (John 3:3);

'...Jesus said, "My kingdom Is not of this world...my kingdom is from another place"' (John 18:36).

The kingdom of God is God's spiritual reign in the hearts of those who love him and in which he saves and indwells his people. Then at a future time he will finish his new creation completely at his Second Coming.[104]

Kingdom revealed; identity concealed

The life of Jesus was so impressive to the gospel writers that they were compelled to write and accurately include material from his teaching as the Holy Spirit brought it back to mind. John, the disciple, took ownership of his otherwise anonymous gospel, 'This is the disciple who testifies to these things and who wrote them down' (John 21:24). He went on to say in conclusion to his gospel, 'Jesus did many other things as well. If every one of them were written down, I suppose that even the whole world would not have room for the books that would be written' (John 21:25). The kingdom of heaven or the kingdom of God is prominent and explicit in the gospels and less so in Acts, the Epistles and Revelation. Jesus did not reveal to everyone in his teaching and in performing miracles who he really was, although the spiritually discerning knew. These included Simeon, (Luke 2:25), John the Baptist (John 1:26-27), Mary Magdalene (Luke 7:37, v50), and Simon Peter [Matthew 16:16-17]. However, there were times when Jesus wanted his identity hidden such as at Caesarea Philippi where in speaking to the disciples, 'Jesus warned them not to tell anyone about him' (Mark 8:30). To the right people at the right time Jesus revealed himself as the Son of God, the Messiah, the King. At other times it was a messianic secret!

He came to be crucified before being glorified. He came to die and be resurrected. He would, after the cross and ascension, gain his throne and be glorified in heaven. That is the whole sequence of steps but between resurrection and ascension something special happened. There were 40 days of intense further teaching in which Jesus taught the disciples about *the Kingdom of God*. At the end of this, as with most of the ordinary people, the disciples still did not understand about the kingdom. That is why we see their confused joint question to Jesus, which we have needed to meet several times in this book, 'Then they gathered around him and asked him, "Lord, are you at this time going to restore the kingdom to Israel?"' (Acts 1:6) On the Day of Pentecost things changed. The disciples then understood about the kingdom! (Acts 2:1-41)

Earthly body; heavenly body

Paul tells the Christians in Corinth that their human bodies are not suitable for heaven. He says, '...flesh and blood cannot inherit the kingdom of God...' (1 Corinthians 15:50). He pointed out that the body is perishable and that we need an imperishable body to be appropriate for heaven. Paul went on to promise that '...we will not all sleep, but we will all be changed' (v51). The restricted earthly body will be replaced by a new heavenly body.

We now enter the realms of Eschatology, the 'part of theology concerned with the final events of history, or the ultimate destiny of humanity.'[105]

From Augustine (354-430), a leading Christian scholar, to the Protestant Reformation (C16th),[106] the arrival of the kingdom had been identified with the formation of the Christian Church. This was not popular with some Christian churches who understood the kingdom of God differently. From the middle of the C20th contrasting eschatological models have been developed which stated that the kingdom had not yet appeared but was still to be started in the future. I believe this is not fully supported by Scripture. Eschatology in Wikipedia suggests:

> 'These diverging interpretations have since given rise to a good number of variants, with various scholars proposing new eschatological models that borrow elements from these.'[107]

Some theologians see another facet in which the kingdom of God is used in Scripture: the literal rule of Christ on the earth during the millennium. Daniel said that '...the God of heaven will set up a kingdom that will never be destroyed...' (Daniel 2:44; 7:14). Many of the other minor prophets predicted the same thing (such as Obadiah v21; Habakkuk 2:14; and Zechariah 14:9). Paul Enns (b.1937), pastor, biblical scholar and writer, tells us that some theologians refer to the future, open manifestation of the kingdom of God as,

> 'The "kingdom of glory" and the present, hidden manifestation of the kingdom of God as the "kingdom of grace." But both manifestations are connected; Christ has set up his spiritual reign in the church on earth, and he will one day set up his physical reign in Jerusalem.'[108]

Kingdom preaching; gospel living

As the Day of Pentecost arrived and the Holy Spirit descended in dramatic appearance, the disciples understood who Jesus was and what his kingdom was. In his growing up alongside them and in his three-year ministry day and night with all of them, it is as if the majority of the time the truth about the person and purpose of Jesus was misunderstood or concealed from them. By the time of Acts (by Luke), and Revelation (by John) and the writing of the Epistles by Paul, Peter, James, John and Jude, the emphasis had moved from kingdom preaching in the gospels to making Christ Lord in the everyday life of the early Christians and in the church. As John Piper says, comparing Gospels with Epistles,

> '"Jesus is Lord" is almost synonymous in the epistles with "the king has come."'[109]

The king *has* come and *will* come. He is Lord and has become Lord in the lives of individuals, but he is yet to reign over everything as Lord and king in the future. The attention must be on the King! He is *the focus* and therefore that fixes the importance of the kingdom.

Prophecy in the Old fulfilled in the New

The Jews were living under occupation and under pressure. Something had to happen. Their nation was God's special family. They knew that but their hope, brought to them through the OT, was for the kingdom to come. This appeared at the time and by the life of Jesus as recorded in the NT. The importance was clear to them, 'He has also set eternity in the human heart' (Ecclesiastes 3:11b). If they could not get restoration by force, which looked impossible because the Romans had conquered and occupied the nation holding it firmly under control, then they thought the Messiah's coming was their opportunity to be released from the Romans.

But they could not see Jesus as being their Saviour from Roman rule or their long-awaited Messiah. They wanted their own kingdom back but not through miracles and parables. Not that way. The kingdom was important, but the majority of Jews could not believe it could happen through Jesus of Nazareth. On the one hand they remarked, '...what is this? A new teaching – and with authority!...' (Mark 1:27) And on the other hand they said, '...we will not have this man to reign over us' (Luke 19:14b KJV). This was made clear by Jesus in the Parable of the ten Minas (Luke 19:11-27) clearly directed at the Jews and at what they were saying.

The Jews wanted the kingdom but on their own terms. Most of us have done this at certain times in life: wanted things on our own terms! I spoke to a neighbour recently just as it started to rain. She said, 'Rain again! We desperately need the rain, but I do wish it would just rain in the night and leave every day with fine weather.' I have also thought the same when out dog walking not anticipating rain only to get soaked a long way from home where my raincoat and umbrella were!

The Jews did believe something would happen and expected a powerful messiah and a warrior king like King David, but not a lowly and gentle Messiah speaking words of love. The OT was quite clear and the many prophesies about the coming Messiah, king or kingdom gave all the details but there was spiritual blindness in the people. For instance, the Bible tells us the Messiah would be from *Bethlehem*, *Egypt*, and *Nazareth*. This is a real enigma. How can anyone come from three places? Yet we read of all three being fulfilled in one chapter in Matthew's gospel.

The wise men visited King Herod in his palace in Jerusalem to see the new baby king, and the Jewish leaders told Herod the Scriptures said the Messiah would be born in *Bethlehem* (as prophesied in Micah 5:2), so Herod sent them from Jerusalem to Bethlehem to find Jesus (Matthew 2:8). Herod was saying he wanted to worship him.

Herod's 'real' but angry motive was to remove the threat to his reign and kill Jesus. This prompted an angel to appear to Joseph and tell him to quickly leave, '...take the child and his mother and escape to *Egypt*. Stay there until I tell you...' (Matthew 2:13). This fulfils the prophecy, '...out of Egypt I called my son' (as prophesied in Hosea 11:1b).

Joseph was told in a second visit to him by the angel whilst in Egypt to go back to Israel, so Joseph and his little family '... went and lived in a town called *Nazareth*. (as prophesied in Isaiah 9:1-2; 11:1) This '... fulfilled what was said through the prophets, that he would be called a Nazarene' (Matthew 2:23).

The coming kingdom was so important God inspired prophets to faithfully deliver the message of the coming Messiah, and hence the kingdom, but the people couldn't see it.

Delivery of King and Kingdom

Jesus did deliver the kingdom and said, '...my kingdom is from another place'

(John 18:36b).

Jesus was the expected King – Pilate saw that and arranged for that to be written over the cross on which Jesus died '...Jesus of Nazareth, the King of the Jews'

(John 19:19).

Jesus also exercised the power to raise himself from the dead, which the spiritually blind could not see, but the spiritually enlightened could see. Jesus said,

'...some who are standing here will not taste death before they see that the kingdom of God has come with power'

(Mark 9:1).

The editors of Encyclopaedia Britannica report in their article by Albrecht Ritschl on Eschatology and The Coming Kingdom of God:

'Thus, Christians were perplexed when the end of the world did not occur within a generation.'[110]

Though Christians were confused when the end of the world did not occur in their lifetime, they came to realise that the establishing of the church was all part of it. They reflected on the life, death, resurrection and ascension of Jesus and realised that there were blessings and challenges for now and a task of sharing the gospel that others might come to faith. This is ever a task unfinished. Rev. Frank Houghton (1894-1972) wrote a hymn to sum up the challenge. It begins:

'Facing a task unfinished
That drives us to our knees,
a need that, undiminished,
rebukes our slothful ease,
we who rejoice to know you
renew before your throne
the solemn pledge we owe you
to go and make you known.'[111]

8 Living as a citizen of the kingdom

John Calvin (1509-1564), a French theologian, pastor and reformer based in Geneva during the Protestant Reformation said it is the task of the church to make the invisible kingdom visible. We do that by living in such an open and honest way that we bear witness to the kingship of Christ in our jobs, our families, our schools, our retirement and our bank accounts because God in Christ is King over every one of these spheres of life. As the Encyclopaedia Britannica puts it:

> 'The kingdom of God, or kingdom of heaven, as the spiritual realm over which God reigns as king, is the fulfilment on Earth of God's will. Though the phrase itself rarely occurs in pre-Christian Jewish literature, the idea of God as king was basic to Judaism.'[112]

Within the Christian faith, especially in relation to living in the kingdom, if Christ is King, he must also be Lord. The only way the kingdom of God is going to be manifest in this world before Christ comes again is if we proclaim it and live it as citizens of God's kingdom and subjects of the King. The psalmist said, 'Let the redeemed of the Lord say so, whom he hath redeemed from the hand of the enemy' (Psalm 107:2 KJV). The questions, therefore, are: What should we speak about? How should we live? What priorities do we hold? What are our values? What are our goals?

Citizenship involves loyalty

Every authority that exists has been established by God (Romans 13:1) even if we don't like the resulting governments! King Nebuchadnezzar declared of the government of Israel by God, 'His kingdom is an eternal kingdom; his dominion endures from generation to generation' (Daniel 4:3b). If God has allowed our government, which after all is temporary, we would do well to compare it with his government or kingdom, which '...will be on his shoulders...' (Isaiah 9:6) and is permanent. In other words, on the shoulders of Jesus, the King. It is therefore reasonable that God expects loyal service of the people he saves by his grace. In the exploration of qualities and priorities, such as loyalty and perseverance, we must look at Revelation as our main source of information on Christian living.

The book of Revelation gives us a good insight into the seven churches in Asia Minor on the circular trade and delivery route (like the British Royal Mail have delivery routes). The apostle John was conscious of the churches covenant relationship with God and so he wrote to encourage them to remain loyal to God throughout the challenges they faced. He wrote to the Christians in Pergamum for instance, 'I know where you live – where Satan has his throne. Yet you remain true to my name' (Revelation 2:13a). He wanted them to remember all the kindness God had shown them, as well as the blessings God made freely available. To those at Thyatira, he wrote, 'I know your deeds, your love and faith, your service and perseverance, and that you are now doing more than you did at first' (Revelation 2:19). He expected them to respond positively and live in faithful obedience to God.

However, stretching across the Mediterranean area, Christians faced temptation towards idolatry including being required by the Roman Empire as its subjects to worship Roman gods and the Emperor to avoid punishment from the government. There was also pressure from Judaism on Christians to abandon their faith in Christ. Judaism was given a special exemption from pagan worship and, at first, Christianity was covered by this exemption. But, as Judaism and Christianity moved apart, this exemption ceased to apply to the Church. This tempted the weaker Jewish Christians to abandon their new faith and return to traditional Judaism in order to avoid opposition and persecution from Rome.

It was particularly challenging being a Christian in the first and second centuries. Some Christians throughout the Roman Empire, when under pressure, compromised their faith by engaging in pagan practices and sexual immorality. They encouraged others into sin with them. It was hard in Asia Minor remaining loyal to the new faith, so John wrote to encourage these first- and second-generation Christians to be loyal to God and to be faithful citizens of the kingdom.

Citizenship involves perseverance

Perseverance can be as simple as remaining faithful to God in belief and actions despite temptation, opposition or discouragement. It involves overcoming obstacles and maintaining faith in God. This is why John brought a challenge to each of the seven recipient churches of his letters (Revelation 2 and 3). This same challenge to persevere is seen through the rest of the book (Revelation 14:12; 18:4; 21:7; and 22:11) and is a theme through the NT. Perseverance is one of the most prominent topics in the book which rounds off the NT and the special challenges faced towards the end of the first century.[113]

Christian citizens overcome through faith in God and through their testimony, loyalty and perseverance. Whatever the challenge is, a promise comes at the end of Revelation where God himself says, '...to the thirsty I will give water without cost from the spring of the water of life. Those who are victorious will inherit all this, and I will be their God and they will be my children' (Revelation 21:6b, v7).

Citizenship involves faith

Faith is described as, '...confidence in what we hope for and assurance about what we do not see' (Hebrews 11:1). It can be a positive trait to have as a Christian when things in our lives seem to be going wrong: when members of your work team are unco-operative; when the children are embarrassing us by their behaviour in church services; when the bank has charged us for yet another letter telling us our account is overdrawn; when a cake being baked sinks in the middle; when the car parked outside won't start on a cold frosty morning. (I have met all these things!) At those times it is difficult to trust God and continue to believe in his sovereignty. This is where the writers of the NT shared their faith and common experience to encourage Christians under pressure, especially when faith was failing.

The Christian life can be very tough. Early believers had difficulty in business. They were persecuted by the government and the church didn't offer them anything satisfying like the worldly pleasures they used to enjoy before becoming Christians.

Faith also includes a steadfast love for God which must be kept alive and strong. 'And without faith it is impossible to please God because anyone who comes to him must believe that he exists and that he rewards those who earnestly seek him' (Hebrews 11:6). The Christians in Ephesus were rebuked for losing their first love (Revelation 2:4). This failure was so great that God threatened to remove this faithless church. A loss of faith, particularly in Christian circles such as in the church, meant a loss of their distinctive witness to the world.

Citizenship involves principles

Acts tells us the four basic principles of how the Early Christians lived. We read, 'They devoted themselves to the apostles' *teaching* and to *fellowship*, to the *breaking of bread* and to *prayer*' (Acts 2:42). (*Emphasis mine*) This had a profound impact on everyone around them particularly as people saw how these new Christians were living. The next verses are also an insight into their personal and public lives.

> 'Everyone was filled with awe at the many wonders and signs performed by the apostles. All the believers were together and had everything in common. They sold property and possessions to give to anyone who had need. Every day they continued to meet together in the temple courts. They broke bread in their homes and ate together with glad and sincere hearts, praising God and enjoying the favour of all the people. And the Lord added to their number daily those who were being saved' (Acts 2:43-47).

95

There was no room for compromise and no place for self-centredness. Towards the end of Acts 4 we come back to details of their lifestyle and we are told of their unity, unselfishness and generosity (Acts 4:32-37), but by Acts 5 we are given insight into a lack of unity amongst the believers as deception and dishonesty creeps in.

Ananias (not the mentor with Paul at his conversion) and his wife Sapphira tried to deceive the apostles and God himself. Peter, the leading apostle, sensed Satan was behind the deception[114] and challenged first the husband and then the wife. They both separately recognised the enormity of their sin and fell down and died. Because of news of this deception and death, 'Great fear seized the whole church and all who heard about these events' (Acts 5:11).

Christianity was spreading at a fast pace, which was alarming to the traditional Jews, especially the Sanhedrin, the leaders in Jerusalem. Peter and John were hauled into prison because of preaching about Jesus and his resurrection and a note-worthy detail in Acts tells us that the number of Christian men had now reached 5,000 and this did not include women and children! They were definitely noticed! When Caiaphas, the High Priest, interviewed Peter and John the next day they immediately brought to the attention of the High Priest '...the name of Jesus Christ of Nazareth...' and said, 'Salvation is found in no one else, for there is no other name under heaven given to mankind by which we must be saved' (Acts 4:10, v12). Salvation could not be found through Caesar or any other source in the first century and it could not be achieved through any other name since. The provision of salvation in Jesus and holding to that truth was, and still is, a vital principle of citizenship.

Another principle is moral purity. 'To the pure, all things are pure; but to those who are corrupted and do not believe, nothing is pure...' (Titus 1:15a); and in Revelation, Jesus rebuked the church in Laodicea for worldliness because they valued wealth and comfort over their loyalty to Christ. We read that their faith had failed them (Revelation 3:14-22).

Faith also involves standing firm in doctrine. Stephen Tong (b.1940), a remarkable Chinese evangelist and theologian explains:

'Doctrine is the basis of service, like a tree whose roots are underground and invisible. Many people see its branches and fruit, but they don't see how the root influences that fruit. Many shallow Christians today don't focus on doctrinal issues, but serious Christians know that doctrine is the basis of everything - it's very important.'[115]

Citizenship involves trials

Christians are encouraged to continue to show loyalty, perseverance and faith and to maintain their principles in the face of trials. There are practical steps in the NT which show us, as in all of Scripture, that the people of God must continue in faithfulness and obedience to what they know and to what has been revealed to them. They are called to be strong through their community, to stay together, to believe together, to testify together and to worship together, as Jesus said in prayer to his father, '...that they may be one as we are one' (John 17:11b). Whatever the context and despite any persecution, the focus must be on what God wants his people to do every day, whether things are easy or tough, and to live holy lives. Jesus said, 'I have told you these things, so that in me you may have peace. In this world you will have trouble. But take heart! I have overcome the world' (John 16:33). Even in the most critical of circumstances, the Christian citizens of the kingdom will receive God's grace and must speak in the name of Christ. In being addressed by the Sanhedrin and told not to speak, 'Peter and John replied... "As for us, we cannot help speaking about what we have seen and heard"' (Acts 4:19-20). Christians are to live in such a distinctive way that their responses to evil are different from those who are not in the kingdom. These are those who do not have Christ as Saviour, and who are excluded from citizenship, '...and foreigners to the covenants of the promise, without hope and without God in the world' (Ephesians 2:12).

Christians must make every effort to be faithful to God, and to persevere in that faithfulness throughout life, and throughout history, until Jesus returns to make all things new. Sadly, many earthly powers, groups and individual people choose to oppose God and so God's people suffer. That can make life really stressful and unhappy. But we must remember that even when life looks discouraging, God is still in control. He is still king in his kingdom.

I have a Christian relative who for quite a time set a mobile phone alarm to go off at mid-day every day. When I first heard it and asked why, the reply was 'To remind me God is still on the throne and has everything under control. When it goes off, I breathe in the presence of God.' What a great reminder of truth!

The darkness of present difficulties and opposition will eventually be replaced by joy and victory at the Second Coming of Christ into his kingdom to take all things under his own control. Now that we have seen how the NT, and the book of Revelation in particular, exhorts the maintenance of loyalty, persevere, faith and principles of holiness in the face of trials, we must also see how the faithful Christian writers encourage us to express our faithfulness in worship.

Citizenship involves worship

Again, we must look into the book of Revelation and see that, as Steve Brown put it:

> 'Despite the fact that John's original audience was suffering great persecution, the book of Revelation has a remarkable emphasis on worship. Revelation 4 and 5 describe an amazing scene of worship in the heavenly throne room, with twenty-four elders seated on thrones surrounding God's throne, and four living creatures flying in the throne room and praising God. Similar scenes of worship occur in over half of Revelation's twenty-two chapters.'[116]

There is a clear connection between suffering and worship. We may think it is impossible or even inappropriate to worship God whilst in pain; this is not usually the case. I know that when I am in distress or pain, physically or emotionally, I cry out to God because he is always there and I believe always interested in me and my circumstances. He is always holy and good and what he does is always perfect. 'We know that in all things God works for the good of those who love him, who have been called according to his purpose' (Romans 8:28). If we go on a little further into Romans 8, we read amazing words from Paul to suffering Christians in Rome which explain our true position when in the most challenging of circumstances:

'Who shall separate us from the love of Christ? Shall trouble or hardship or persecution or famine or nakedness or danger or sword? As it is written: "For your sake we face death all day long; we are considered as sheep to be slaughtered." No, in all these things we are more than conquerors through him who loved us. For I am convinced that neither death nor life, neither angels nor demons, neither the present nor the future, nor any powers, neither height nor depth, nor anything else in all creation, will be able to separate us from the love of God that is in Christ Jesus our Lord' (Romans 8:35-39).

This is why we must continue to worship God. We always consider God to be worthy of our worship, remembering that worship is actually 'worth-ship'. 'You are worthy, our Lord and God, to receive glory and honour and power' (Revelation 4:11a); '...Praise and glory and wisdom and thanks and honour and power and strength be to our God for ever and ever...' (Revelation 7:12). One reason we worship is because of the words of the elders who addressed Jesus, described as the Lamb, in relation to God's people, 'You have made them to be a kingdom and priests to serve our God, and they will reign on the earth' (Revelation 5:10). Citizenship and reigning with Christ truly does cause us to express our gratitude, praise and thanks in worship.

Citizenship involves witness

A practical example of witness is seen in the book of Acts. The Ethiopian queen's treasurer, a eunuch, went to Jerusalem to worship. He was no doubt a spiritual man, a Jew, or a convert to Judaism. An angel told Philip, the disciple, to go to the road from Jerusalem to Gaza. When he got there, the Holy Spirit gave him exceptional running speed to join the chariot of the official on his return journey towards Ethiopia and ask him if he understood what he was reading from the book, or scroll, of Isaiah which he had picked up from the temple.[117] The official invited Philip into his chariot to explain to him who Isaiah was talking about. Philip then, 'meeting' the Ethiopian at the point where he was, used this OT book to explain the good news of Jesus.[118] The official told his driver to stop and said, 'Look, here is water. What can stand in the way of my being baptized?" (Acts 8:36b). We can presume that Philip had a clear grasp of the gospel and explained it well bringing the official to want to become a Christian and want to show his new faith by being baptised. We then read that the evangelist baptized the eunuch by immersion in nearby deep water (v38). Following that, God's Holy Spirit took Philip away and the eunuch was full of joy (v39). He had been born-again and taken the step of obedience into baptism. This indicated the washing away of sins, as Ananias told Paul in Damascus (Acts 22:16). This was the time at his conversion and baptism, when Jesus added the Ethiopian to the family of God. He identified with the death and resurrection of Jesus Christ and became a citizen of his kingdom (Romans 6:3-4) by grace through faith.

Citizenship involves prayer

The Lord's Prayer, as encountered earlier, was taught by Jesus to his disciples and serves as a pattern for prayer for all people for all time. Luke has the shorter version (Luke 11:2-4), and Matthew, as part of the Sermon on the Mount, the longer one (Matthew 6:9-13). As with other prayers in the NT, it links with the hearers' Jewish background and, after simple introductory words, uses the basic elements of Jewish prayers: praise, petition, and a longing for the coming of the kingdom of God.[119]

Jesus taught the disciples what would happen in the near future and that they would have grief but then promised it would turn to joy. He told them, '...in a little while you will see me no more, and then after a little while you will see me' (John 16:16). He then went on to pray what we might call the High Priestly prayer (John 17). John would have been with him and would be challenged by what Jesus said and so he recorded it for us in his gospel. He tells us Jesus prayed to be glorified (v1-5); he prays for his disciples (v6-19); and he prays for future believers (v20-26).

As the Lord's Prayer set the template, this prayer sets the principles, so that believers, that is citizens of the kingdom, might have the best example for prayer that is possible.

We find there are other prayers, calls to prayer or examples of people praying in the NT worthy of our attention. The following is just a selection of prayers addressed to God but always prayed for a reason, as prayer should be so central and so vital to Christians in their new citizenship.

Matthew

(Praying in secret)

'But when you pray, go into your room, close the door and pray to your Father, who is unseen...'

(Matthew 6:6)

Mark
(Praying in faith)

'Therefore I tell you, whatever you ask for in prayer, believe that you have received it, and it will be yours.'

(Mark 11:24)

Luke
(Praying during an important event)

'When all the people were being baptized, Jesus was baptized too. And as he was praying, heaven was opened.'

(Luke 3:21)

John
(Praying in the name of Jesus)

'You may ask me for anything in my name, and I will do it.'

(John 14:14)

Acts
(Praying constantly)

'They all joined together constantly in prayer, along with the women and Mary the mother of Jesus, and with his brothers.'

(Acts 1:14)

(Praying last words)

'While they were stoning him, Stephen prayed, "Lord Jesus, receive my spirit." Then he fell on his knees and cried out, "Lord, do not hold this sin against them." When he had said this, he fell asleep.'

(Acts 7:59-60)

(Praying in desperate circumstances)

'Peter sent (*the mourners*) out of the room; then he got down on his knees and prayed.'

(Acts 9:40a) (*Emphasis mine*)

Romans
(Praying in the Spirit)

'In the same way, the Spirit helps us in our weakness. We do not know what we ought to pray for, but the Spirit himself intercedes for us through wordless groans.'

(Romans 8:26)

Corinthians
(Praying within marriage)

'...devote yourselves to prayer...'

(1 Corinthians 7:5)

Galatians
(Praying as you leave one another)

'The grace of our Lord Jesus Christ be with your spirit brothers and sisters. Amen.'

(Galatians 6:18)

Ephesians
(Praying and giving thanks)

'I have not stopped giving thanks for you, remembering you in my prayers.'

(Ephesians 1:16)

Philippians
(Praying with joy)

'In all my prayers for all of you, I always pray with joy.'

(Philippians 1:4)

Colossians
(Praying to know God's will)

'...we have not stopped praying for you. We constantly ask God to fill you with the knowledge of his will...'

(Colossians 1:9)

Thessalonians
(Praying for God's blessing on your work)

'...we constantly pray for you, that our God may make you worthy of his calling...'

(2 Thessalonians 1:11a)

Timothy and Titus
(Praying night and day)

'... night and day I constantly remember you in my prayers.'

(2 Timothy 1:3b)

Philemon
(Praying for others)

'I always thank my God as I remember you in my prayers.'

(Philemon v4)

Hebrews
(Praying with confidence)

'Let us then approach God's throne of grace with confidence, so that we may receive mercy and find grace to help us in our time of need.'

(Hebrews 4:16)

James
(Praying in trouble, when happy, and when sick)

'Is anyone among you in trouble? Let them pray. Is anyone happy? Let them sing songs of praise. Is anyone among you ill? Let them call the elders of the church to pray over them...'

(James 5:13-14)

Peter
(Praying with a clear mind)

'The end of all things is near. Therefore be alert and of sober mind so that you may pray.'

(1 Peter 4:7)

John
(Praying in God's will)

'This is the confidence we have in approaching God: that if we ask anything according to his will, he hears us. And if we know that he hears us – whatever we ask – we know that we have what we asked of him.'

(1 John 5:14–15)

(Praying for good health)

'Dear friend, I pray that you may enjoy good health and that all may go well with you...'

(3 John v2)

Jude
(Praying a hymn of praise – doxology)

'To him who is able to keep you from stumbling and to present you before his glorious presence without fault and with great joy – to the only God our Saviour be glory, majesty, power and authority, through Jesus Christ our Lord, before all ages, now and forevermore! Amen.'

(Jude v24-25)

Revelation
(Praying prayers offered to the Lamb – Jesus)

'...the four living creatures and the twenty-four elders fell down before the Lamb. Each one had a harp, and they were holding golden bowls full of incense, which are the prayers of God's people.'

(Revelation 5:8)

Citizenship involves lifestyle

Living with taxes

Disciples of the Pharisees and the Herodians tried to trap Jesus in his teaching by challenging him about his views on paying taxes to the Romans whom they hated as occupiers of their country (Matthew 22:15-22). Jesus saw through their actions and rejected their superficial flattery, under-lying intentions to trap him and their hypocrisy. He called for a Roman coin and from its Imperial image and inscription pointed out that they had a moral duty to pay taxes to Caesar and to give to God what is rightly his. This silenced his accusers who then at least had the humility to withdraw. We learn from this teaching supported by a visual aid that Christians have a responsibility to be good citizens of an earthly kingdom (Romans 13:1) and to be good citizens of the heavenly kingdom in which it can be right to obey God rather than people when there is a clash (Acts 5:29).

David Landrum, director of advocacy at the Evangelical Alliance in the UK, cautions and advises us about Romans 13 that it,

> '(*gives*) us guidance for being good citizens: paying taxes, obeying the law, and respecting the author-ities, etc. However, problems sometimes arise because, although God (his nature, his word, and his holiness) is unchanging, human ideas of citizen-ship are not. So, as fashions, trends and appetites change, the dominant set of ideals and beliefs of a particular time is exalted above the will of God.'[120] (*Insertion mine*)

Christians must follow Christ's teaching and example and keep the balance of commitment to God and the state right. Jesus did not attempt to reform human government nor use political means to overthrow it. He preached the need to enter his kingdom on God's terms.

Living with politics

Jesus told Pilate that his kingdom is not of this world (John 18:36), and that it is not achieved through politics or by military action. The world is Satan's kingdom, and Christ came not to reform Satan or improve his handiwork, but as the angel said to Joseph, '...give him the name Jesus, because he will save his people from their sins' (Matthew 1:21), and so save people from Satan, his kingdom and his control. Christians are citizens of the kingdom of God and '...no longer foreigners and strangers, but fellow citizens with God's people and also members of his household' (Ephesians 2:19). The kingdom and eternal life are begun on earth in citizenship, but the complete reward or 'inheritance,' as Peter called it, is 'kept' (NIVUK) 'reserved' (KJV) in heaven, (1 Peter 1:4). This fact means that Christians must create distance between themselves and the world with its social, political, economic and religious affiliations and compromising complications (2 Corinthians 6:14, 17). We live subject to human laws, as we saw with the Imperial coin illustration, *and* by God's laws, but if and when they clash, we must remember we cannot serve two masters (Matthew 6:24).

Living with national pride

Jesus told the parable we call The Parable of the Tenants (Matthew 21:33-41). This is followed by an application by Jesus which led to a severe reaction from the Pharisees (v42-46). The parable features a vineyard and this would have been captivating to the Pharisees who had their national and personal pride at heart. Jews have their three national tree symbols: the olive, the fig and the vine. As a nation they held to the comparison of being like a vineyard (Isaiah

5:1-7) and would look upon this parable and interpretation by Jesus with great interest. However, what they heard made them fiercely angry. They knew he was comparing the rejection of the prophets in their history to them and could see where he was going in the killing of the vineyard owner's son (yet to happen to Jesus, but they were thinking about it).

Jesus made it clear that the vineyard owner expected fruit and thereby financial profit, but his requests to send him what was his were met with a harsh response and rejection by the tenant workers in charge of the vineyard. They were in no doubt that the parable was directed at them and so we see that in their evil hearts they harboured murderous thoughts in their humiliation. The leaders in Israel had political and religious power and authority but realised Jesus was saying that the kingdom would be taken away from them and given to others who *would* be fruitful and obedient. Some of the words clearly upsetting the Pharisees were, 'Therefore I tell you that the kingdom of God will be taken away from you and given to a people who will produce its fruit' (Matthew 21:43). In other words, the Jews would lose and the Gentiles would gain the favour of God: the kingdom! There is no wonder the Chief Priests and Pharisees wanted to silence Jesus!

Living with a new nature

Jesus said that 'Flesh gives birth to flesh, but the Spirit gives birth to spirit' (John 3:6). This is why we call it being 'born again' (v7). This is the result of being called by God to receive his eternal life by repentance and faith and to be saved through grace. It is a precious gift to a sinner. It is forgiveness and the imparting of a new nature. At birth we received from our parents their nature, what Paul refers to as '...our flesh...following its desires and thoughts' (Ephesians 2:3). When we are born again, we receive from God *his* nature, and so we, '...participate in the divine nature...' (2 Peter 1:4). This is the new nature that citizens of the kingdom of God have received and learn to live with. In the first chapter of the Bible (Genesis 1:21), as the Forerunner Bible Commentary tells us,

> 'The Bible shows that a fundamental law of nature is that every living thing brings forth its own kind. What is produced by a vegetable is vegetable; what is born of animal is animal. What is born of sinful man and woman is a sinful child, which Paul designates as being '...the realm of the flesh...' (Romans 8:8). It cannot be anything else. We may educate it and cultivate it all we please, but human nature remains 'flesh.' It may be refined flesh, beautiful flesh, or religious flesh, but it is still 'flesh.'[121]

Paul makes a contrast with the realm of the flesh by introducing life in the realm of the spirit (Romans 8:9-17). Those born of God are spiritually alive, as Paul told the Christians in Rome, and he also shared the same truths with the Christians in Corinth (1 Corinthians 2:9-16). Every born-again person is automatically at that instant a child of God and a citizen of the kingdom of God. By the time Paul wrote again to the Corinthians in his second letter to them, he explained that '...in Christ, the new creation has come: the old has gone, the new is here!' (2 Corinthians 5:17)

How to become a citizen of God's kingdom

Kingston

At the secret but precise time and as scheduled, the news was passed from person to person: 'The Queen has arrived!' This was Tuesday 25 June 2002 when I worked in a special educational setting with pupils with complex learning and physical disabilities. It was then I met Queen Elizabeth II. It was when she was touring Britain to celebrate her Golden Jubilee on the throne, having become Queen in 1952. One place she visited was the Royal Borough of Kingston upon Thames, London, where I worked at the time. 2002 was also the 1100th anniversary of the coronation of Saxon King Edward the Elder in 902 and she was due to visit All Saints Parish Church in Kingston. It is an ancient church built on the spot where the Saxon kings were crowned using the Kings Stone (from which Kingston gained its name). Eight Saxon kings were crowned there and in the year 925 the tribes and regional kingdoms in the land combined to form England at Kingston as a united country for the first time.

Security for the late Queen's visit was intense with armed police on roof tops, helicopters circling overhead, divers searching the Thames and the Queen had a sizeable entourage. With poise, dignity and attendants, she walked into the Parish Church. (The route having been 'swept' by the police). I had the briefest conversation with her as she approached me near the church entrance. She recognised that I was heading up a team and each of us as staff supported one to one our severely disabled wheelchair-using pupils. As she passed, she said to me, 'This must be a special school.' I answered her as per instructions upon first time of being spoken to and said, 'Yes, Ma'am,' and she walked on. It was a fairly low-key ceremonial visit. There are times when she processed surrounded by absolute majesty, riches and splendour such as at the annual State Opening of Parliament (in which nearly all the years of her reign, she had been the focal point). Compared to that, this occasion was dignified but simplified.

Heaven

None of these British regal occasions, simple or complex, will compare with the riches and splendour of heaven. I am humbled and proud to have spoken to Queen Elizabeth II as a British citizen and just as humbled and just as proud and thankful to be a citizen of heaven. Perhaps one day I will speak to the new monarch, King Charles III?

The first citizenship is temporary. The second is eternal. One day I will speak to Jesus, the King of kings and Lord of lords – and I look forward to a conversation with him!

Proof of citizenship

Citizenship of heaven, the centre of the Kingdom of God, can be certain and secure. I am sure of my position as a Christian citizen of heaven and so was John Bunyan (1628-1688), a Puritan non-conformist preacher and writer (and tinker by trade), languishing for 12 years in Bedford jail for preaching what the authorities did not want to hear: the gospel. He was kept there because he refused to give up his faith. He had endless time and restrictions as a result of his imprisonment, but a heart in tune with God, so at God's prompting he wrote about a fictitious character he called Christian in his allegorical book Pilgrim's Progress.[122] It is regarded as one of the most significant works of religious, theological fiction in English literature. It has been translated into more than 200 languages and has never been out of print from the time it was written by Bunyan in 1678. The main character had a scroll which he was instructed to carry through his life's journey and he was warned not to lose it. This certificate indicated his new birth and new life and was to prove, when shown upon arrival, to be the means of his entrance into the Celestial City.

If I travel overseas, and at other times when official government authorised documentation is needed, I can show my British passport which proves I have British citizenship. Could I have had citizenship conferred on me before I was born? Could I become a citizen when I was merely conceived? The answer is No and No! Nations register children *after* they are born, not while still in the womb. Once I was born, my father registered my birth with the authorities in my part of South Yorkshire in Northern England.

Paul tells the Christians at Philippi, 'Our citizenship is in heaven...' (Philippians 3:20a). We enter the kingdom by being 'born again' (John 3:5-7). Those who try to enter in other ways are unable to do so. Assorted reasons for exclusion are listed as Paul writes to Corinth and reminds Christians who is excluded from the kingdom of God (1 Corinthians 6:9-10), concluding with the words, 'And that is what some of you were...' (v11a).

Nicodemus, a judge becomes a Christian

A good example of a person becoming a citizen of the kingdom of God is seen in Nicodemus who had an encounter
with Jesus. Later references to him in the NT show this led to
a life changing experience. He may well have been afraid ini-
tially of the reactions of his colleagues, so he came to Jesus
under cover of darkness. He had a position and reputation to
guard, but he also had a great feeling of unrest in his heart
and questions to which he wanted answers.

Nicodemus was a Pharisee and member of the greater
court of the Sanhedrin and therefore a leader of the ruling council of the Jews nationally, equivalent to being an
experienced and respected senior Member of the British
parliament or judiciary.[123] He is mentioned three times in
the Gospels.

The *first* mention was a meeting at night to discuss
with Jesus his teachings (John 3:1-15). Jesus went straight
to the heart of his need and challenged Nicodemus about
being born again. Jesus knew he needed a complete change
of mind and life. Nicodemus asked of Jesus very reasonable
questions about being born when you are old and showed at
that point he could not understand the spiritual dimension
of the new birth.

The *second* mention was when he reminded his Sanhedrin
colleagues (who were critically dismissing the Jewish 'guards'
and the 'mob' as being uneducated), that their law requires
that a person be heard before they are judged (John 7:46-51).
The Sanhedrin had likened Jesus to the ordinary people and
Nicodemus was not going along with that but was defending the right of Jesus to be properly heard and understood
before they judged him. By now Nicodemus had gained in

knowledge of salvation and confidence to live out what he had learned and was able to confront colleagues with his application of the Jewish law and, in doing so, protect his new friend Jesus from spurious accusations and arrest and trial at that stage (v32, v43-44). He appealed to Jewish practice, justice and common sense, even though other Pharisees were critical of Nicodemus in doing so and made disparaging remarks about Galilee.

The *third* and final mention was after the crucifixion of Jesus to provide embalming spices and to help Joseph of Arimathea in preparing the body of Jesus for burial and then laying Jesus to rest in the garden tomb (John 19:38-42). By now, he was putting his life 'on the line' for the One who had become his Saviour: his Messiah. I believe there are all the signs in these references that he had come to faith and become a citizen of the Kingdom.

The new birth

To be a Christian means to be saved and this is achieved by the new birth: being born-again. Jesus left no doubt about it when he emphasised to Nicodemus: '...You must be born again' (John 3:7b). We must now see what is meant by birth: physical and spiritual.

The physical birth experience

There are three important phases connected with a birth of a baby:

(1) creating,
(2) delivering,
(3) living and maturing as a result of that process.

To look further,

(1) the father passes the seed into the mother where it combines with her egg;
(2) at full term, the baby is delivered by the mother;
(3) the baby begins to live in relationships within its birth family and enjoy pleasures, privileges and challenges as they arise.

The spiritual birth experience

There are three similar stages of development:

(i)   challenging,
(ii) believing and receiving,
(iii) living and maturing with Christ as Lord.

To look further,

(i)   the Spirit is implanted by grace into the human heart and is fed by the word of God, the gospel;
(ii) it is received by repentance towards God and faith in Jesus as Saviour by the individual;
(iii) this then leads to acknowledge Christ as Lord and the aim is to live a holy life honouring to him.

This spiritual birth is a perfect Divine plan and course of action but may not be, for everyone, as simple and straight-forward as described. However, the amazing and wonderful fact is that the person has come to know the King and become a citizen of the Kingdom of God. Christ is '...the head of the body, the church...' and *(has)* '...the supremacy' (Colossians 1:18). (*Insertion mine*) He is '...the ruler of the kings of the earth' (Revelation 1:5b). A person going this route has been born-again and is now in the Kingdom, which in Colossians is referred to as the body of Christ: the church.

The role of the Holy Spirit

The NT makes it clear that the Holy Spirit always works in the process of new birth, often through the Bible, the word of God. This, in the experience of the Early Church, was through '...the apostles' teaching...' (Acts 2:42) which would be their recollection of the teaching of Jesus, combined with their Scriptures which we call the OT. James in his letter says, 'He chose *to give us birth* through the word of truth, that we might be a kind of firstfruits of all he created' (James 1:18). (*Emphasis mine*) Peter said something similar, 'For you have been born again, not of perishable seed, but of imperishable, through the living and enduring word of God' (1 Peter 1:23). Having come to new birth through the work of the Holy Spirit, individuals need to learn how to walk in the Spirit; how to be led by the Spirit; and how to enjoy the kingdom of God, according to David Pawson.[124]

The outcome of new birth: citizenship of the Kingdom

As Jesus declared to Nicodemus the goal of the new birth is entrance into the kingdom of God (John 3:5). This kingdom is the church (Matthew 16:18). '...the church...is his body...' (Ephesians 1:22; Colossians 1:18, v24): the body of Christ. This is salvation put simply and the Holy Spirit is at the centre of the conversion of each individual.

Kings and priests

Right now God reigns on his throne in heaven and he calls his people on earth to be his kingdom of priests. We see this in the words of Steve Brown, Professor of Practical Theology at Reformed Theological Seminary, Orlando, Florida:

> 'In the Old Testament, both kings and priests were highly honoured because they had been chosen by God to represent him in his relationship with his covenant people. But they were allowed to prosper in these honoured offices only as long as they were loyal to God. At the present time, God reigns on his throne in his heavenly temple. And he calls his people on earth to be his kingdom of priests.'[125]

Though only a select few in the OT were chosen as kings and priests, the Scriptures looked forward to a day when all of God's faithful people would be both kings and priests on the earth. In being a king, to reign; in being a priest, to offer up worship. As God told Moses, '" Now if you obey me fully and keep my covenant, then out of all nations you will be my treasured possession. Although the whole earth is mine, you will be for me a kingdom of priests and a holy nation." These are the words you are to speak to the Israelites' (Exodus 19:5-6a). It is because of the presence and ministry of Jesus on earth that John in Revelation tells us this special day is already here. 'You have made them to be a kingdom and priests to serve our God, and they will reign on the earth' (Revelation 5:10). Paul tells Christians, the church, you are to '...offer your bodies as a living sacrifice, holy and pleasing to God – this is your true and proper worship' (Romans 12:1).

119

Our royal position

God told Moses that he had chosen Israel to be a royal Imperial priesthood. This language in Exodus is taken by Peter in the NT and used to refer to the church, 'But you are a chosen people, a royal priesthood, a holy nation, God's special possession, that you may declare the praises of him who called you out of darkness into his wonderful light' (1 Peter 2:9). In many respects this sounds strange, because when we think of OT priests, what we normally think of is that priests do just a limited number of things; they offer sacrifices on behalf of the people, they pray and lead prayer and they may blow trumpets and take part in ceremonial celebrations. However, the Bible is actually saying that God-inspired activity on earth is an act of being a royal priesthood for those who serve God and are in his kingdom. In the same way, everything we do as Christians is to be done heartily as if for the Lord no matter how simple or mundane. Whatever it is, if it is an activity done in holiness as by a royal priest, we are acting responsibly and in gratitude to God for all he has done for us and as one of his ambassadors on earth. We are appointed to minister to him and to others and to offer to him our constant and sincere worship. This lifestyle as a citizen of his kingdom carries with it great honour and great responsibilities.

Our worship

All this reminds us that in our relationship with him we can bring him boundless joy in the way we obey him, worship him and live our life faithfully to our calling, as Paul told the Ephesians, '...lead a life worthy of the calling you have received' (Ephesians 4:1). It is the faithfulness, fruitfulness and obedience constantly covered by prayer that brings happiness and joy to God.

Our prayers

God is vitally interested in what we are and what we do. He watches intently when we serve him and listens attentively to us when we pray. He even uses our prayers as means through which he blesses others and when the time and circumstances are right to bring healing to ourselves and others. He stands with those who are persecuted and supports those who are distressed, alone or feel forsaken. He judges and stands against those who oppose his reign.

It is indeed an honour to serve God, whether we regard ourselves as priests, ambassadors, or simply as a Christian citizen of the kingdom into which we have come. We have now been anointed for the task of spreading the gospel of this kingdom and of ministering to God himself as we do so, as well as bringing blessing to others around us as we serve them. In our relationship with our God, we find he listens to us as we pray and in his sovereignty, he may even change circumstances for which we are praying. If he does, we are commanded to keep praying. If he does not, again we are commanded to keep praying. One day in heaven I believe we will find out why some of our prayers did not appear to be answered on earth as mysteries are explained to us (1 Corinthians 13:12). Our prayers will certainly be poured out before God, (Psalms 141:2; Revelation 5:8; 8:3-4). Paul told the Christians in Thessalonica, 'Rejoice always, pray continually, give thanks in all circumstances...' (1 Thessalonians 5:16, v17, v18a).

Not only is the past forgiven for citizens of the kingdom, but the present is full of challenge and change and requires commitment. God has promised to bless us now and in the future.

Future Blessings

Palm branches

In the OT palm branches were routinely used in the Feast of Tabernacles. It indicated celebration because God would bring victory or salvation (Leviticus 23:40). When John records that Jesus entered Jerusalem during his triumphal entry, again we see palm branches used by the crowd to welcome him, which showed they believed that he was bringing deliverance and the messianic kingdom of God (John 12:12-13). Further on in the NT we also read of palm branches being used in celebration where there was, '...a great multitude...standing before the throne and before the Lamb. They were wearing white robes and were holding palm branches in their hands' (Revelation 7:9). Here the palm branches carried by this multitude indicate that the people had received the future blessings of God's kingdom. They expressed their thanks for these blessings in worship with the angels (v10-12).

Rewards

If you are part of his kingdom then you have inherited eternal life and that will last forever. This is the greatest reward: knowing that you will spend eternity in the presence of the King of kings and enjoy his kingdom. This is the ultimate reward of being a citizen of God's kingdom and what a wonderful reward this truly is!

The 24 elders in Revelation provide us with an example of active worship and reward, or blessing, to come. In the presence of God, they are respectfully on their thrones and fall forwards in worship giving thanks to God because of who he is and was and because he has begun his reign. On one hand the elders say it is the time to reward prophets and God's people (Saints), (Revelation 11:16-18); on the other hand, John also sees the future day of judgement, '...destroying those who destroy the earth' (v18e).

Jesus - unchanging

Looking to the past and especially to victory achieved by Jesus on the cross, Christians can take heart for the future knowing because Jesus was victorious over his enemy, we shall also be victorious over the same enemy and over our trials.

If we die now there is the blessing of going straight to heaven. As Paul told the Corinthian Christians, 'We are confident, I say, and would prefer to be away from the body and at home with the Lord' (NIVUK), '...absent from the body... present with the Lord' (KJV) (2 Corinthians 5:8). If Jesus returns before we die, there is the blessing of being part of the new heaven and the new earth which is linked with his coming. This gives great encouragement to praise and worship God and I feel sure we shall be almost overwhelmed by the splendour and glory, more than anything we can imagine. 'However, as it is written: "What no eye has seen, what no ear has heard, and what no human mind has conceived" – the things God has prepared for those who love him' (1 Corinthians 2:9). We worship God for what he has done in the past, what he is doing in the present and for what he will do in the future, 'Jesus Christ is the same yesterday and today and forever' (Hebrews 13:8). He is unchanging and so should our desire to worship be unchanged and unceasing.

This gives hope and confidence, even in the tough times, for the citizens of the kingdom. God remains faithful and says, '...Never will I leave you; never will I forsake you' (Hebrews 13:5; based on Deuteronomy 31:6).

What Does It Mean to Be a Citizen of God's Kingdom?

Rights and privileges for you as a citizen

Clarence L. Haynes Jr., writer, speaker and author, addresses citizenship of the kingdom with its rights and privileges in the following words:

> 'As a citizen of a country, you are granted certain rights. For example, you have the right to vote, the right to work, and the right to pay taxes (even though that is a right I would gladly give up if I could). Regardless of where you live or grow up, if you belong to God, you are also a citizen of the kingdom of God.'[126]

God's Lordship for you as a citizen

To be a citizen of the kingdom, we must enter by choice; we are never forced by God to enter. Then as a member of God's family we submit to his Lordship if we want the full blessing of our position in Christ. We can resist and even be ignorant of the facts or know and reject the facts – both are possible (as I have seen from experience)! The guidebook and instruction manual for our new position is, of course, the word of God. If we apply what we read there it gives God the authority over our life. This is the essence of what Paul writes to the Christians in Rome, 'Therefore, I urge you, brothers and sisters, in view of God's mercy, to offer your bodies as a living sacrifice, holy and pleasing to God – this is your true and proper worship' (Romans 12:1).

As a kingdom citizen we compare our ambitions and life-style with what we read in the Bible and choose to make Christ our Saviour, Lord and King. If we do not live this way, we are not truly under his authority or submitted to him. One of the saddest things I read in the Bible is in a parable Jesus told.

A nobleman went off to a foreign land to be crowned king. Before he could return his servants 'sent a delegation after him...' and the sad words are in their message to their master, '...We don't want this man to be our king' (Luke 19:14b). These people with this attitude would not deserve to be citizens of the kingdom of God. Sadly, this is the position with people who reject Jesus and therefore his kingdom. There is a saying about his position in our life, 'If he is not Lord of all, he's not Lord at all.' Over the years I have longed for Christians to come into full commitment in their faith by making Christ Lord, but it has met with resistance by some people. I have also longed for this for myself, and I have to admit I have often fallen short of God's glory, 'for all have sinned and fall short of the glory of God' (Romans 3:23). Often Christ has not occupied the central position in my life of which he is worthy.

In recent dark winter months I have been watching a box set of films based on the day-to-day politics of the White House. On so many occasions I heard the phrase, 'I serve at the pleasure of the President.' Yes, you do as an employee and faithful member of his team. Equally, we serve at the plea-sure of Jesus our King of kings. What he says we must do, but as a pleasure and not as a chore! 'Jesus said to his disciples, "Whoever wants to be my disciple must deny themselves and take up their cross and follow me"' (Matthew 16:24).

God's protection for you as a citizen

One special blessing of being a citizen of God's kingdom is that you live and work under God's protection. When the Jews challenged Jesus about whether or not he was the Messiah, he spoke of believers, members of his kingdom, as being his 'sheep' and said, 'I know them'...'no one will snatch them out of my hand' (John 10:27-28). Jesus said to God, his Father:

> "I have revealed you to those whom you gave me out of the world. They were yours; you gave them to me, and they have obeyed your word.... they believed that you sent me. I pray for them... for they are yours.... they are still in the world, and I am coming to you. Holy Father, protect them by the power of your name, the name you gave me, so that they may be one as we are one. While I was with them, I protected them and kept them safe by that name you gave me"' (John 17:6, v9, v11-12a).

Paul was convinced of our secure salvation and protected position in Christ, and so emphatically told the Christians in Rome,

> 'For I am convinced that neither death nor life, neither angels nor demons, neither the present nor the future, nor any powers, neither height nor depth, nor anything else in all creation, will be able to separate us from the love of God that is in Christ Jesus our Lord' (Romans 8:38-39).

In Christ, we are truly protected and safe.

God's provision for you as a citizen

As with many people in Britain my wife and I have a dog. It is not anyone's dog; it is *our* dog and we are responsible for her and for providing for her all that she needs. This has not always been the case. She is five years old, but the first half of her life was lived in Cyprus and for most of it she was on the street living on her wits, quite wild and answerable to no one. Furthermore, as far as we know, no one provided anything for her. Eventually, she was rescued by a charity and then brought to the UK where she is now our dog. We are her owners and she is secure and appears to be happy. Now, when it comes to a mealtime, she cannot open a tin of dog meat herself. She cannot even get a tin or some dog mixer biscuits out of the cupboard. She may be hungry, but her paws are not designed to open tins and cupboards! We do all that for her. She is protected. She is provided for. Furthermore, she does not worry about meals. They are all provided. Every day!

If you are a citizen of God's kingdom, then the king is responsible for your provision. His resources are available to you as your resources. Since you belong to him, he will use his resources to take care of you. As with our dog, you do not have to worry about your provision. It will come to you from a loving Father who loves to provide for his own children. When Jesus gave the finest sermon ever preached by anyone, the Sermon on the Mount (Matthew 5-7), he said:

> 'So do not worry, saying, "What shall we eat?" or "What shall we drink?" or "What shall we wear?" For the pagans run after all these things, and your heavenly Father knows that you need them. But seek first his kingdom and his righteousness, and all these

things will be given to you as well. Therefore do not worry about tomorrow, for tomorrow will worry about itself. Each day has enough trouble of its own"' (Matthew 6:31-34).

As a kingdom citizen our responsibility is to humbly let Jesus be Lord. I say again this is the practice of submitting to the Lordship of Christ. When you do this, he has promised to make every provision for you.

In the poem by Elizabeth Cheney (1857-1940), 'The Robin and the Sparrow' we read:

'Said the robin to the sparrow,
"I should really like to know,
Why these anxious human beings
Rush about and worry so."
Said the sparrow to the robin,
"Friend I think that it must be,
That they have no heavenly Father,
Such as cares for you and me."'[127]

The poem speaks for itself. As one of my wife's elderly relatives used to say in simple faith when things were tough, 'Trust in the Lord'!

God's purpose for you as a citizen

King Solomon was one of the wisest people who ever lived. That was his reputation over a vast area of the Middle East. He had enough wealth to cushion him from the challenges of life and he had enough time to observe people and the world around him. He used some of his time to write amazing books with wise sayings in them including Proverbs and

Song of Songs (Song of Solomon). He also probably wrote Ecclesiastes which includes eight well-known verses beginning with, 'To everything there is a season, and a time to every purpose under heaven' (Ecclesiastes 3:1 KJV).[128]

'Time' and 'purpose' are linked in these verses. One of the most important things to *do* and *be* as a citizen of God's kingdom is to surrender to God's purpose. It is so important to trust him to reveal his will to us individually and then to carry out his wishes. No matter how small or simple his requests seem to be. You will notice I said '*do*' and '*be*' as a citizen or Christian. It is good to be active in the service of God but he sometimes, in my experience, wants us to 'be' and not rush round and worry so much and 'do' so much to fill our time which is partly to impress others because we want them to notice. I know this to be true now I have retired and have had to learn to slow down and relax.

To find God's purpose for our lives I think the easiest way is to listen to him. It is a challenging thing to do as we often feel more comfortable speaking, as we do in prayer, instead of listening for his voice deep inside our hearts and minds whilst in meditative prayer. But it is a good discipline to be quiet and tune-in to him. According to the saying, 'We have one mouth and two ears, so we should spend twice as much time listening as speaking.' As God said through the psalmist, 'Be still and know that I am God...' (Psalms 46:10a). In stillness we can listen. In listening we can hear God speak.

There are four practical things we can do to find God's purpose for our lives. These have been encountered earlier in our studies but here I bring them together:

1. Look deeply into God's word, the Bible;
2. Seek out like-minded Christians for fellowship;[129]

3. Meet with others for 'breaking of bread' (Communion) and worship;
4. Pray. Pray on your own. Pray with others. Pray in your mind. Pray aloud. Pray your own words. Pray the words of others.

The first disciples or Apostles set the example to the Early Church. We have met the following references but it is necessary to say them again: 'They devoted themselves to the apostles' teaching and to fellowship, to the breaking of bread and to prayer' (Acts 2:42). We should do what God asks us to do because we want to do his will on earth. As we pray in the Lord's Prayer, '...Your will be done...' (Matthew 6:10). This should be the purpose and desire of every citizen of the kingdom of God.

10 Looking Ahead

The kingdom has witnesses

The Bible teaches that to become a citizen in the Kingdom one must be born again! Once this has happened, the sincere and committed Christian who trusts Christ as Saviour and wants to mature in their faith, the person who relies on the infilling of the Holy Spirit, the person who believes in the truth being in God's word, the person who puts holiness first in their life, that person will steadily grow more like Christ and be a worthy citizen of his kingdom. They may also respond to the challenge to be a clear witness to others including to take the step of baptism as a sign to all that they have received forgiveness of sins (Acts 2:38; 22:16) and intend with God's help, to live their new life. People may be critical of Christians in their midst but they cannot fail to see this witness, that a person – their friend, work colleague, neighbour or relative – has been born again and has a peace and joy and a new lifestyle. They just cannot deny what they see!

The kingdom is completed

In the second coming of Christ he returns as a triumphant king to take full control of his kingdom. As he returns to achieve final victory in the war against Satan, 'On his robe and on his thigh he has this name written: King of kings and Lord of lords' (Revelation 19:16). The time has come for all his enemies to be overcome and he will reign in his kingdom and over the citizens of it. There will be the new heaven and new earth and a righteous reign. His first coming at his birth established his kingdom and his second coming in triumph and glory will complete it. The kingdom of God was, is and will always be, central to the ministry of Jesus. The OT writers knew of God's eternal reign, 'The Lord reigns forever...' (Psalm 146:10a). These words are employed by John in the NT, '...he will reign for ever and ever' (Revelation 11:15c). They were also used by Handel in his Messiah oratorio. The Creed used by the Church of England (often, the Nicene Creed), based on that agreed by the First Council of Nicaea in 325 AD proclaims this truth of eternity and tells us,

'...his kingdom will have no end.'[130]

The kingdom is now

Despite all that has been explained and all we see written in God's word, certain people put off a decision to become a born-again Christian. They are influenced by apathy, by busyness and by religion, which is stale, stilted and superficial. By religion, I am not thinking of real Christian faith: the real Christian life, living in the kingdom as born-again believers or citizens. There is a significant difference between religion which is informative, ritualistic and academic, and real life, which is centred on the person of Christ, the filling of the Spirit and living with the values and message of the kingdom. So many people refuse a commitment and prefer to leave things for later. This includes religious people who live defeated, destitute and spiritually dead existences. David said, 'Taste and see that the Lord is good...'

(Psalms 34:8a). Jesus said, '...I have come that they may have life, and have it to the full' (John 10:10b).

The kingdom is unique

When one of my young grandchildren says grace, in a private home or in a public restaurant seated inside or outside, that little one says in a very loud voice, 'Thank you God for all your love; thank you for all your grace; thank you for all this food. Amen.' That is putting it simply. It is simply correct, and a joy to hear a four-year-old witness to truth and thankfulness. As citizens of the kingdom and believers in Christ, we can also accept and put things simply. We are to know him, love him and worship him as Lord. This recognises his reign. We are to live out his teaching and live in anticipation of his return. Without complicating things, when Jesus taught his disciples how to pray, part of the instruction and example was to pray that God's kingdom would come in fullness on earth. He said, 'Your kingdom come, your will be done, on earth as it is in heaven' (Matthew 6:10). The kingdom has been established but is not yet complete and that is what we are told to pray for.

The writer, Courtney Whiting adds,

'As members of God's kingdom, through Christ, we are ambassadors of God on earth (2 Corinthians 5:20). Our role as ambassadors is to proclaim the good news of the kingdom of God.'[131]

The kingdom is waiting

The kingdom is waiting for individuals to enter it. The question here is, 'How long will it take for you to decide to enter God's way?' I have heard an incredibly wise and clever theologian say that the following words of Jesus cause him to tremble because of the depth of the challenge and truth in them. 'For I tell you, that unless your righteousness surpasses that of the Pharisees and teachers of the law, you will certainly not enter the kingdom of heaven' (Matthew 5:20). Jesus went on to say in the Sermon on the Mount, 'Not everyone who says to Me, "Lord, Lord" will enter the kingdom of heaven, but only the one who does the will of my Father who is in heaven' (Matthew 7:21). Later, speaking again to the disciples he says, '... unless you change ('are converted' KJV) and become like little children, you will never enter the kingdom of heaven' (Matthew 18:3). A person *can* enter into God's Kingdom, *but it has to be God's way!*

The kingdom is the church

We are all familiar with the chapter of parables in Matthew 13 in which every parable begins, 'The kingdom of heaven is like...' (Matthew 13: 24, v31, v33, v44, v45, v47, and v52). Jesus then illustrates a matter that directly involves instruction in things of the kingdom and for its citizens: the church and its members. In doing this, he is using the term 'kingdom of heaven,' but he could have said 'the church' – he is regarding the terms as equal and interchangeable. This is because born-again members of the church are the citizens of the Kingdom of God. In Jesus' parable of The Weeds it is noticeable that angels are named as the ones who gather the weeds, not just from any group of people in society, but from amongst and alongside those who are in Jesus' kingdom. Weeds seem to have fellowship with them! When Jesus talks with a scribe who makes wise insightful comments

(Mark 12:28-34), he says to him, 'You are not far from the kingdom of God' (v34). He can see that the scribe is thinking so deeply and sincerely that he is near to being converted and becoming a citizen of the kingdom: a member of the body of Christ, the church. Jesus was the expert in this earthly ministry searching for those who were themselves searching for the kingdom.

The kingdom and the harvest

My front lawn has looked extremely attractive to my wife and I and to people passing by. The grass on it is two years old and has been faithfully supplied with grass feed and watered in dry periods. It has been a deep green and almost weed free – *until recently!* Now it has a fair distribution of weeds. Where did *they* come from? I have no idea, but in Winter the grass is resting. The weeds are certainly unwanted, but Winter is the wrong time of year to get rid of them without seriously disturbing the grass, so I shall just have to wait until Springtime when the grass begins to grow again and then treat the lawn and remove the weeds.

This parable is unusual in that it is recorded in two instalments. In the first part, Jesus was speaking to his disciples and the general public. It gives us the details of the crop being planted and at night an enemy comes and sows weeds amongst the wheat. The farmer was quite convinced there was an enemy working against him. The second part of the parable comes later. Later in the day. Jesus was now inside the house away from the crowds and the confused disciples asked him for an explanation about the parable. If a parable by definition is '*an earthly story with a heavenly meaning,*' then Jesus gives the heavenly or spiritual meaning specifically to his disciples. He says *he* scattered the seed. The field is the world. The good seed represents the people or citizens of the kingdom. They live alongside those who assume they are citizens but, sadly, have never been born-again. They are individuals who have not accepted Christ as Saviour. We read that the weeds are people planted by Satan amongst those in the kingdom. The harvest is the end of the age and the harvesters are the angels. At the harvest, the two crops will be sifted and sorted. The bad crop of those who do not accept Christ as Saviour will go, as Jesus said, '...into the blazing furnace...' but for the citizens of the kingdom, '...the righteous, will shine like the sun in the kingdom of their Father...' (Matthew 13:42-43)[132]

This is a very sober story which requires no further explanation.

The kingdom and the returning King

In this book we have explored aspects of the kingdom. We began with a simple Windsor chair which once belonged to a man who became an Emperor for a day and we end with a royal throne for a King who will reign for eternity. The hope of all Christians is that one day our King will return and reign on Earth. He will reign from his throne. This hope motivates us to endure and to overcome every trial we experience in life. No matter what hardships and persecution we face because of our faith, we show our loyalty to God and Christ as our king because we know that his word is truth and we believe it. Jesus will return to reign over us and his kingdom, and to reward us. Until that happens, we trust in the promise of his final words at the end of Revelation, 'He who testifies to these things says, "Yes, I am coming soon."

(*and John replies*), Amen. Come, Lord Jesus' (Revelation 22:20). (*Insertion mine.*)

I trust I have met my aim presented in the Introduction to this book to answer questions about the King and the Kingdom: who the King is and what the Kingdom is. We have moved through the development of the monarchy, through the physical to the spiritual and from the OT and into the NT. We have held closely to Scripture as our principal and infallible authority. We have assessed the Values of the kingdom and the Message of the Kingdom. We have looked at a selection of facets of the Spiritual Kingdom and looked at what is meant by the Importance of the Kingdom. This led us to look at what it should be like Living as a citizen of the Kingdom and how to *become* a citizen of the Kingdom. Lastly, in this chapter, 'Looking Ahead,' we have thought about the return of the King to his Kingdom and the ensuing harvest. Interwoven in all this, we have seen the kingdom is the Church and thought of our place in this and other life experiences we find ourselves in and facing varied tests and joys which God allows.

The kingdom and God's plan

I trust you feel that God has a plan for you as I believe he has for me. God's words of encouragement to Jeremiah, a really burdened prophet, stand for you and me for all time, '"For I know the plans I have for you," declares the Lord, "plans to prosper you and not to harm you, plans to give you hope and a future"' (Jeremiah 29:11).

It is my prayer that you, the reader, might be encouraged and blessed as a result of your reading *The Kingdom* and that God might receive the honour and praise from all our hearts for presenting to us his kingdom. To use the words of Jesus at the end of the Lord's Prayer: 'For yours is the kingdom and the power and the glory forever. Amen' (Matthew 6:13b).[133]

Charles Wesley (1707-1788) recognised that at the point of birth Jesus was already King. He was not born a prince waiting to become a king. He wrote in that famous and popular hymn, 'Come thou long expected Jesus,'

> Born thy people to deliver,
> Born a child and yet a King,
> Born to reign in us forever,
> Now thy gracious kingdom bring.[134]

...and finally

As I reach a conclusion, I would like to refer to the words of one of the criminals crucified with Jesus which I find extremely challenging. As thieves and convicted criminals they were led out to crucifixion with Jesus (Luke 23:32). Like Jesus, they had also received the death penalty. One was a God-fearer. I look forward to meeting him one day! You may like to consider my assessment of the situation:

> He was nailed to a cross and about to die;
> He had no chance of a reprieve;
> He initially insulted Jesus, before reconsidering;
> He chose his last words carefully;
> He appealed to Jesus – from his position an arm's length away;
> He could have complained about his circumstances, but he didn't;
> He could have asked Jesus to somehow set him free, but he didn't;

He could have cursed Jesus or kept quiet, but he didn't;
He gave a heart-felt plea of a sinner wanting mercy;
He challenges us all by his attitude and humble words.

The criminal said,

'Jesus ('Lord' – KJV) remember me when you come into your kingdom' (v42).

'Jesus answered him,

"Truly I tell you, today you will be with me in paradise"'(v43).[135]

May God bless us each one, bring us into the kingdom *now* by faith through his grace and keep us looking for the kingdom in all its fullness *to come*. Amen.

Endnotes

1. The grand daughter, who had a flat in Fulham, was the Head Teacher at a London school. I was one of her two Deputy Heads.
2. The chair is a Windsor English twelve spindle stick-back chair with a solid elm seat. It dates from about 1800. It is not a valuable antique but as would be reported on the long-running BBC Antiques Roadshow (from 1979), the provenance makes it unique and adds to its value.
3. In 2014, in her annual Christmas Day address to the UK and Commonwealth, Queen Elizabeth II said that the life of Jesus was an inspiration and an anchor in her life. She said: "Jesus Christ lived obscurely for most of his life, and never travelled far. He was maligned and rejected by many, though he had done no wrong. And yet, billions of people now follow his teaching and find in him the guiding light for their lives. I am one of them because Christ's example helps me see the value of doing small things with great love."
4. Lewis Carroll; Through the Looking Glass; Macmillan; 1871.
5. OT is Old Testament and NT, New Testament as explained on the Contents page, note 3.
6. 'Jesus shall reign' reflects an 18th century vision of the world church. It uses the language of Psalms 72:8 and Ephesians 1:20-21. Isaac Watts paraphrased this psalm in ways that reflected his time and the geo-political position of England and the rise of the British Empire. It first appeared in his collected work: *Psalms of David*. How could a paraphrase of an OT psalm mention Jesus? Watts believed that the Psalms reflected Christian experience and regarded Psalm 72 as just that and so as a Christological reference he links it with Ephesians 1.

Endnotes

7. www.knowing-jesus.com/topics/Kingdom-of-God; 2021.

8. References are taken from the New International Version of the Bible, Anglicised, referred to as NIVUK: The New International Version; Biblica; 1973, 1978, revised 1984 and 2011.

9. References appear in the familiar format of book, chapter, verse, (as in John 3:16). If already referring to John chapter three, then reference to a verse will be indicated as, for example, (v16). Occasionally there may be reference to KJV: King James Version; 1611. Other versions, where used, will be explained.

10. John Blanchard; What in the World is a Christian; Evangelical Press; 2014, p130.

11. Genesis 1:26-30.

12. The Bible is quite clear that the sin of Adam and Eve has passed to all people for all time, 'For all have sinned and fall short of the glory of God' (Romans 3:23).

13. John David Pawson; Kingdoms in Conflict; Anchor Recordings; 2015, p31; (www.davidpawson.org).

14. The Northern Kingdom of Israel was taken to Assyria in 722 BC and the Israelites scattered to various parts of the empire. A remnant remained in the land of Israel, but they became diluted with other local peoples giving rise to groups such as the Samaritans. The Southern Kingdom of Judah was exiled to Babylon under King Nebuchadnezzar. Deportation began about 603 BC, and Jerusalem and the temple destroyed in 586 BC.

15. The books of Ezra and Nehemiah cover this return in 536 BC.

16. The London school mentioned earlier (End notes 1).

17. Ben Dunson, Editor; The Kingdom of God in the Old Testament: Kingship and Creation; American Reformer blog; 14 04 2015.

18. That is: The Commonwealth of Israel from the time of Moses until the election of Saul as king; Oxford Languages Dictionary; Oxford University Press; 2021.

19. en.m.wikipedia.org>wiki.

20. Judges covers the period of 1150-1021 BC.
21. It was unusual in Israel's history for a woman to be a warrior-leader, but she emphatically stated that the Lord would give victory and that the enemy would fall '...into the hands of a woman...' (Judges 4:9b). She acted with leadership, authority and courage. (See: God remembered Rachel; Jenni Williams; SPCK; 2014, where there is an interesting chapter 7 on: 'Deborah: more like a man.')
22. The first three reigns, and a number after that, were of the united kingdom of the twelve tribes of Israel: Saul 1021-1000 BC; David 1000-962 BC; and Solomon 962-922 BC. Rehoboam then succeeded his father, Solomon, but the kingdom divided into North and South in 931 BC. This split became two kingdoms with Jeroboam, an official of Solomon, becoming king of the ten tribes in the North and Rehoboam, son of Solomon, king of the two tribes in the South.
23. Samuel faithfully served God, but as he grew old, he appointed his two sons to lead Israel. They did not have the moral principles or authority of their father and turned from uprightness to accept bribes and pervert justice and this is why the elders put Samuel under pressure to bypass them as judges and appoint a king.
24. Psalm 106 does not tell us the details of this disease.
25. The Editors of Encyclopaedia Britannica; 1768; (Now only published on-line with annual revisions); www.britannica.com/summary/Saul-king-of-Israel.
26. God chose the Israelites in his sovereignty and by his grace. The Bible does not explain more than this. God said to Moses '...I will have mercy on whom I will have mercy, and I will have compassion on whom I will have compassion' (Exodus 33:19b); repeated by Paul to the church in Rome (Romans 9:15). A humorous but serious quip from William Norman Ewer a journalist, with a riposte from his journalist friend, Cecil Browne, in the early C20th puts this in perspective:

Ewer: 'How odd of God to choose the Jews?'
Browne: 'It's not odd for God well knew his Jew!'

27. Solomon began well and enjoyed some success, but soon failures in his reign began to appear. He didn't follow the Lord as his father, David, did and he permitted pagan worship (1 Kings 11:33).

28. The two stages of the exile were firstly 722 BC, (Northern Kingdom), and the second stage started 605 BC (Southern Kingdom) with the exile ending in 536 BC. Most scholars round off the length of the captivity or exile to the Southern Kingdom's 70 years. Whilst the whole of the two kingdoms were taken away as slaves, a remnant of people remained. They were left because of being unable to travel and so they could care for the land. (John C. Whitcomb; Old Testament Kings and Prophets; BMH Books; 1977; bookshop.org/books/chart-old-testament-kings-and-prophets-paper; 2021.) John C. Whitcomb (1924-2020) was professor of theology and Old Testament at Grace Theological Seminary, Winona Lake, Indiana, for 38 years.

29. On 3 April 1968, Dr Martin Luther King Jr., an American Baptist minister and activist who became the most visible spokesperson and leader in the American civil rights movement from 1955 until his assassination in 1968, was encouraging people, especially people of colour, to keep going to the Promised Land in his speech at the Mission Temple, Memphis, Tennessee. His speech was entitled 'I've Been to the Mountain Top.' He included the words 'I just want to do God's will. And he has allowed me to go up to the mountain. And I've looked over. And I've seen the Promised Land. Mine eyes have seen the glory of the coming of the Lord.' Reported in Wikipedia. En.m.wikipedia.org. Edited November 2021.

30. Ben Dunson; The Kingdom of God in the Old Testament: The Prophetic Hope; 13 06 2015; www.ligonier.org/posts/kingdom-god-old-testament-prophetic-hope.

31. The approximate period of Isaiah's ministry was 739-690 BC.
32. See also Isaiah 40:9-11 to see how tenderly God promised to treat his people.
33. The approximate period of Jeremiah's ministry was 627-575 BC.
34. Shepherds were a symbol of kingship.
35. The approximate period of Daniel's ministry was 605-536 BC. This covered the reigns of Nebuchadnezzar and Belshazzar and several shorter reigns of others in between.
36. Belshazzar reigned 553-539 BC.
37. If only the governments of this world would listen to and honour those words and let God and the Lord Jesus Christ reign?
38. Ben Dunson; The Kingdom of God in the Old Testament: The Prophetic Hope.
39. George Frederick Handel (1685-1759) composer, was German until 1715 when he became British.
40. To warn and challenge is still the same role now for Christians today as we witness to what we know.
41. en.wikipedia.org/wiki/Kingdom_of_God_(Christianity).
42. David L. Turner; Matthew; Baker Academic; 2008; p37.
43. R.C. Sproul; The Prayer of the Lord; Ligonier; 2018; www.ligonier.org/learn/articles/what-is-kingdom-god; blog; 13 09 2021.
44. Synoptic is based on the Latin: 'Synopticus' which in turn comes from the Greek for synopsis which means seeing together and is especially applied to the first three of the four gospels - Matthew, Mark, and Luke. John has a quite different and individual approach with his, the fourth gospel. (See: en.m.wikipedia.org/synoptic gospels).
45. English Standard Version; Crossway; 2001, revised 2007, 2011 and 2016.
46. Although we read 5000, this was just the men present. It could well be that there were the same number of women and children, who were not included in this total, so a total

figure could be nearer to 15,000 people who were fed. This would be a significant sized army if they had wanted to press forward with their action (John 6:1-15).

47. Easton's Bible Dictionary; usually referred to as: The Illustrated Bible Dictionary, Third Edition; Matthew George Easton (1823-1894); Thomas Nelson; 1897 (and later revisions).

48. We read in John 3 how Jesus replied to Nicodemus:

v3 'Jesus replied, "Very truly I tell you, no one can see the kingdom of God unless they are born again."

v4 "How can someone be born when they are old?" Nicodemus asked. "Surely they cannot enter a second time into their mother's womb to be born!"

v5 Jesus answered, "Very truly I tell you, no one can enter the kingdom of God unless they are born of water and the Spirit.

v6 Flesh gives birth to flesh, but the Spirit gives birth to spirit.

v7 You should not be surprised at my saying, "You must be born again."'

49. Ezekiel, for instance wrote 'I will give you a new heart and put a new spirit in you; I will remove from you your heart of stone and give you a heart of flesh' (Ezekiel 36:26). This was a new birth and deliverance from the power of sin (Ezekiel 36:25-31). Other major prophets of the OT say similar things: 'Then all your people will be righteous...' (Isaiah 60:21a); and 'I will give them a heart to know me, that I am the Lord. They will be my people, and I will be their God, for they will return to me with all their heart' (Jeremiah 24:7).

50. Blog: bible.org/seriespage/4-kingdom-God-new-testament-continued; 01 01 2008.

51. Blog; Bible.org; Ibid.

52. Luke's reference to Theophilus reminds us, as with his first book, his gospel, how he has conducted careful research based on the evidence of eyewitnesses and their early records

and he locates the activities around the kingdom and Jesus' ministry in the context of world events and secular powers. One of the notable things about both Luke and Acts is that he names local rulers and is careful to get them and their different titles right.

53. Jesus teaches the disciples for 40 days about the kingdom. The number 40 in the Bible signifies a period of preparation. It was forty years in the wilderness God prepared Israel to enter the Promised Land. Jesus spent 40 days in the desert in preparation for his ministry.

54. Their Scriptures or Hebrew Bible is organised into three main sections: the Torah, or Teaching, also called the Pentateuch: the Five Books of Moses; the Nevi'im, or Prophets; and the Ketuvim, or Writings. It is often referred to as the Tanakh.

55. The kings and kingdoms are those depicted by the parts of Nebuchadnezzar's statue, interpreted by Daniel.

56. Arthur Bliss; *Whosoever will*; African Episcopal Church Hymnal; 1870. (The hymn begins: '"Whosoever heareth!" Shout, shout the sound! Send the blessed tidings all the world around; Spread the joyful news wherever man is found: "Whosoever will may come!"')

57. This emphasis on the kingdom therefore tells us: (1) The kingdom and kingship of Jesus is central to the gospel; (2) The Kingdom of God will overcome the kingdoms of the world; (3) The Kingdom is for everyone.

58. Chris Green; The King, his Kingdom, and the Gospel: Matthew, Mark, and Luke-Acts; IVP; 2006. (Especially pages 104-37).

59. Shane Scott is writing in Focus Magazine; www. focusmagazine.org/the-kingdom-emphasis-in-acts.php; 05 10 2017. He also has a blog at www.thinkingthroughfaith.com.

60. Ian Paul, Associate minister of St Nicholas, Nottingham, England; Managing Editor, Grove Books; member of the General Synod; www.psephizo.com/biblical-studies/the-kingdom-of-god-in-acts-1/; 13 05 2020.

61. Chris Green; The King, his Kingdom, and the Gospel in Matthew, Mark, Luke-Acts; IVP; 2006.
62. Living Stream Ministry; The Kingdom in the Acts; ministrysamples.org; 2014.
63. R.H. Boll; The Kingdom of God in The Epistles; (third edition revised 2000); Church of Christ Mission. Also: www.wordandwork.org/2013/08/the-kingdom-of-god-in-the-epistles/; August 2013.
64. R.H. Boll; The Kingdom of God in The Epistles.
65. Righteousness means 'right standing,' 'morally right,' 'justifiable' or 'a work in progress.' Oxford Languages Dictionary; OUP; 2021.
66. Dictionary; Merriam-Webster; 1828 (revised frequently); (now part of Encyclopaedia Britannica), gives the core meaning of revelation:
    i. usually a secret or surprising fact that is made known;
    ii. an act of making something known;
    iii. something that surprises you.
    www.merriam/webster.com/dictionary/revelation#:~:text=1a%20%3A%20an%20act%20of,or%20astonishing%20disclosure%20shocking%20revelations; the meaning of this word updated 06 12 2021.
67. en.wikipedia.org/wiki/Book of Revelation.
68. Witness Lee; Life Study of Revelation (Living Stream Ministry); High Peak Books; 1984.
69. Consider the words used by John as he greeted the churches of Asia Minor: 'John, To the seven churches in the province of Asia: Grace and peace to you from him who is, and who was, and who is to come, and from the seven spirits before his throne, and from Jesus Christ, who is the faithful witness, the firstborn from the dead, and the ruler of the kings of the earth. To him who loves us and has freed us from our sins by his blood, and has made us to be a kingdom and priests to serve his God and Father — to him be glory and power for

ever and ever! Amen' (Revelation 1:4-6). There are numerous references here to God's kingdom in these three verses: God is on his throne; Jesus rules over the kings of the earth; the church is the kingdom that serves God.

70. Greg Perry is Associate Professor of New Testament and Director of City Ministry Initiative, Covenant Theological Seminary, Missouri.
71. Easy to Read Version; World Bible Translation Centre, 1987.
72. John Murfitt; Two Destinies; Zaccmedia; 2022.
73. Steve Brown; The King and his Kingdom; Founder of Key Life Network; Florida; in his blog: thirdmill.org/seminary/lesson.asp/vid/135; 2021.
74. They must have said this very much *tongue in cheek* because they hated Caesar and the Roman occupation. However, the Jewish leaders hated Jesus more and were happy to get the ordinary people excited against Jesus!
75. In John 5, v3b and v4 are missing from certain manuscripts so the NIVUK and some versions do not include them, but the KJV and others do.
76. The Chinese have been 'taking the waters' since the C7th BC; The British in Tunbridge Wells from 1606, in Bath 1690 and in Matlock from 1698.
77. The disabled man's healing of body and soul came through the words of Jesus.
78. Jews accepted that God worked on the Sabbath sustaining his creation, but they could not bear to hear that in calling God his Father in the way he did, Jesus was inferring his equality with God.
79. This saying was used by Hilary Hinton, "Zig" Ziglar (1926-2012) American author, salesman, and motivational speaker with a Christian faith; https://en.wikipedia.org/wiki/Zig_Ziglar. A.A. Milne used the question in Winnie the Pooh, published 1926, but Pooh's answer to Piglet was 'You don't spell love, you feel

it!' The phrase was around before Zig Ziglar and A.A. Milne used it.

80. Phillip Bliss became an itinerant music teacher on horseback in Winter and attended an academy of music in New York each Summer. He was converted at a Revival aged 12 and eventually became a singing evangelist at Revivals in later life until he died.

81. Four Corner Ministries; Jesus' message of the Kingdom of God; https://www.biblicaltraining.org/library/ethics-kingdom-god/ biblical-theology/van-pelt-blomberg-schreiner; 2021.

82. Matthew was one disciple using his own material, and Mark who seems to have received his source material from Peter, another.

83. Biblical author source material is beyond the scope of this present book.

84. By the time the wise men arrived, Jesus would be a toddler nearly two years old. His mother and stepfather took him from Bethlehem to Egypt for safety to escape from Herod's slaughter and then the family returned to Nazareth (Matthew 2:16, v19, v23).

85. Phillip Bethancourt; Ten Connections Between Jesus and the Kingdom of God; (For more information on misunderstanding Jesus); https://erlc.com/multi_author/phillip-bethancourt; 24 02 2014. Phillip Bethancourt is executive vice president of the Southern Baptist Convention and assistant professor of the Southern Baptist Seminary, Texas.

86. In *Italic* are words omitted from some manuscripts.

87. R.T. Kendall; The Sermon on the Mount; Monarch; 2013; p231.

88. 'father' in this reference (Mark 11:10) is David.

89. Salem Web Network, Richmond, Virginia, provides Christian content and interactive tools to help people understand Christianity. They are a conservative Protestant group. See:

The Kingdom of God? Understanding Its Meaning. Christianity. com; Editorial Staff; 30 Jan 2019; www.christianity.com/god/what-is-the-kingdom-of-god-understanding-it-s-meaning.html.

90. James M. Hamilton Jr; www.ligonier.org/learn/articles/kingdom; (Working with Prof. N.T. Wright); 01 11 2011.

91. Walter A. Elwell, General Editor; The Evangelical Dictionary of Theology; Baker Books; 1984, revised 2001.

92. Figuratively speaking, the dragon represents Satan. The woman is Mary, and the baby is Jesus. Another dimension is also represented here, that is the opposition from Satan to the work of God and the gospel, as well as to the people of God in their witness.

93. David Seemuth working with Rt. Revd. Prof. NT Wright, of the UK., (Regarded as one of the world's leading New Testament scholars). David Seemuth is a Professor at Trinity International University, specialising in the New Testament. www.ntwrightonline.org/the-gospel-and-the-kingdom-of-god/; 2020.

94. Taylor Hampton, Solicitors; Advice on becoming a British Citizen; London; 2021.

95. Becoming a Kingdom Citizen; www.kingdomcitizens.org; 2012.

96. Certain Bible verses do not draw a distinction between soul and spirit but speak of body and soul (Matthew 10:28), or body and spirit (James 2:26). Other verses have all three: body, soul and spirit (1 Thessalonians 5:23).

97. Possibly and probably King Solomon (971-931 BC).

98. Arthur Campbell Ainger was born in Blackheath, London, and educated at Cambridge University before teaching at Eton College for 37 years.

99. Cortney Whiting studied at Dallas Theological Seminary. She is currently a Church lay-leader and writes for various Christian ministries. Her blog is: Unveiled Graces; www.ibelieve.com/meet-our-writers/cortney-whiting.html.

100. en.m.wikiquote.org.
101. English Standard Version; Crossway; 2001, revised 2007, 2011 and 2016.
102. John Piper; The kingdom of God; Founder and Teacher, desiringGod.org; www.desiringgod.org/interviews/what-is-the-kingdom-of-god; 08 09 2017.
103. Cortney Whiting studied at Dallas Theological Seminary.
104. The Second Coming cannot be covered in this work, so the present writer will simply commend it as a definite future event.
105. This concept is commonly referred to as *The end of the World* or *End Times*. This theological concept first appeared in English around 1844. (Oxford English Dictionary; OUP; 1857 and later revisions).
106. This major movement within Western Christianity is generally accepted to have been started by Martin Luther (1483-1546). He was an Augustinian monk who became a professor, writer and priest. He taught that salvation was by faith through grace alone and not by works which made him very unpopular with his church. After heart-searching, he nailed his 95 theses to the church door at Wittenberg, Germany in 1517. As a result, and because of his unflinching position, he was excommunicated from the Roman Catholic church by Pope Leo X in January 1521, and citizens were banned from defending or propagating his ideas from May of that year.
107. Eschatology; en.wikipedia.org/wiki/Kingdom_of_God_(Christianity); 21 09 2021. (These alternative theories cannot be covered in this present study).
108. Paul B. Enns; Moody handbook of theology; Moody Press; 1989. (www.gotquestions.org/kingdom-of-God.html. 26 04 2021).
109. John Piper; The kingdom of God.
110. The Editors of Encyclopaedia Britannica; www.britannica.com; Eschatology.

111. Rev. Frank Houghton was ministering in England but was challenged by Hudson Taylor's missionary service in China and so he joined the China Inland Mission in 1920. He wrote this hymn in 1909.

112. The Editors of Encyclopaedia Britannica; Kingdom of God: Christianity.

113. Most early theologians (such as Irenaeus in 180 AD), say the book of Revelation was written in the rule of the Emperor Domitian (81-96 AD), and it reflects the persecution of Christians in that period, particularly referring to the evil Emperor Nero (54-68 AD). They say that 'the Beast' (Revelation 13:17), and the number '666' (Revelation 13:18), refer to him. Together with more recent theologians, the most common date for publication of Revelation by John is 95 AD.

114. Peter confronted Ananias saying, '...you have lied to the Holy Spirit' (Acts 5:3).

115. Rev. Dr. Stephen Tong is the Pastor of a megachurch in Indonesia, promoter of the Reformed Evangelistic Movement, the founder of the Stephen Tong Evangelistic Ministries International, and the Reformed Evangelical Church and Seminary in Indonesia; en.wikipedia.org/wiki/Stephen Tong.

116. Steve Brown; The King and his Kingdom.

117. This was rather like we might purchase a guidebook whilst visiting a National Trust property and read it on the way home. The eunuch could not be a complete convert to Judaism as the Mosaic law forbade it (Deuteronomy 23:1). Greeks called them *half-men*. The passage he was reading was Isaiah 53:7-8.

118. Philip was sharing the gospel in his witness to this stranger.

119. https://www.britannica.com/topic/Roman-Catholicism/The-liturgy-of-the-Word - ref931982.

120. David Landrum; Dual citizenship: The will of government and the will of God; Evangelical Alliance; (www.eauk.org/news-and-views/God's-kingdom-and-our-dual-citizenship); 26 04 2018.

121. Bible Tools blog; Forerunner Bible Commentary; 2021. www. bibletools.org/index.cfm/fuseaction/topical.show/RTD/cgg/ ID/14165/Citizens-Kingdom-God.htm.

122. John Bunyan; The Pilgrim's Progress from This World to That Which is to Come: delivered under the similitude of a DREAM; Nath Ponder Press; 1678; (en.m.wikipedia.org.).

123. The Sanhedrin was the Jewish court of 70 senior Jews or Rabbis, and a president. They were the judges in the post-exilic days and functioned as the Supreme Court: the *Great Sanhedrin*. When needed as judges, they sat as a tribunal and tried the most serious national alleged law-breaking cases throughout the land of Israel. The lower court was the *Lesser Sanhedrin* of 23 Jewish judges. They tried the lesser and local cases. (wikipaedia.com.)

124. John David Pawson; Kingdoms in Conflict; p117.

125. Steve Brown; The King and his Kingdom; Founder of Key Life Network, Inc., a teaching ministry that uses radio broadcasts, podcasts, seminars, and publications; thirdmill.org/seminary/lesson.asp/vid/135; 2021.

126. What Does It Mean to Be a Citizen of God's Kingdom? clarencehaynes.com.; www.biblestudytools.com/bible-study/ topical-studies; 23 10 2021.

127. Elizabeth Cheney; The Robin and the Sparrow; www. goodreads.com/quotes/714001-the-robin-and-the-sparrow-said-the-robin-to-the; (Elizabeth was the daughter of Mormon pioneers and lived in Utah); This poem is thought to be based on an earlier one of 1508 called 'Phyllyp Sparowe' written and published by John Skelton.

128. It has also been made into a song with a very endearing tune: 'Turn! Turn! Turn!' (To Everything There Is a Season); Written by Pete Seeger and sung by The Byrds; 1965.

129. As someone said, 'Fellowship is fellows in a ship.' If the ship is a small boat and there are two of you, then you only have each other and you must get on!

130. Christian leaders met at Nicaea in 325 AD. The Creed was agreed so that common beliefs were agreed. It was revised by the First Council of Constantinople in 381 AD. This Nicene Creed was included in the Prayer Book issued and authorised by Archbishop Cranmer (1662) and has gone through additions and revisions, such as the Book of Common Prayer (1979) and Common Worship (2000).

131. Cortney Whiting; What Is the Kingdom of God? 10 Things Christians Need to Know; Blog; Ibelieve.com/faith/What Is the Kingdom of God? 01 10 2018. (Courtney is writing here for Ibelieve.com. and Salem Web Network, California).

132. For the full story of The Parable of the Weeds, see: Matthew 13:24-30, v36-43.

133. There is doubt in the minds of some whether this final phrase of the prayer was in the original Greek NT, but it is a suitable concluding doxology (benediction or blessing), and sounds like the actual words of Jesus, according to R.T Kendall (b.1935) American evangelist and English Pastor, who adds, 'After all, the words are absolutely true, even if Jesus did not say them' (R.T. Kendall; The Sermon on the Mount, p263).

134. Charles Wesley (1707-1788) was an English clergyman, author, and hymn-writer, who, with his brother John, and George Whitfield, founded the Methodist movement. He wrote more than 6500 hymns. (en.wikipedia.org/wiki/Charles Wesley).

135. Though he was himself dying, Jesus still had time to answer the convicted criminal who wanted to be remembered. He was very much aware of eternal life and that he and Jesus were passing into it. Matthew and Mark tell us that at first both robbers insulted Jesus. We are also told that the God-fearing one points out the innocence of Jesus to his fellow criminal, (indicating his understanding of Jesus and his facing of reality) and admits to Jesus that he knows Jesus will shortly arrive in his kingdom. I believe this points to a man who has come to personal faith, in that he addresses Jesus as Lord (Luke

23:42 KJV) and that he knows Jesus is the King going to his Kingdom. '...no one can say Jesus is Lord except by the Holy Spirit' (1 Corinthians 12:3b). See the full story of the thieves at the Crucifixion: (Matthew 27:38, v44; Mark 15:32; Luke 23:32-33, v39-43; John 19:18, v32). The words of the criminal, 'Jesus remember me when you come into your kingdom' (Luke 23:42), were used by a Frenchman, Jacques Berthier (1923-1994) and formed into a harmonised Taizé chant in 1978.

About Me

John is enthusiastic about the subject of this book as with his first, Two Destinies, published by Zaccmedia, 2022. After extensive research, The Kingdom is a subject which he is burdened to share.

His past includes experience in the ministry, education, and family life; meeting the challenges all these have presented.

He lives near the South coast of Cornwall and in his retirement attends local churches, enjoying DIY, dog walking, and keeping and breeding Pekin bantams. He likes writing and occasionally he plays golf.

He has been married to Ruth for more than fifty years and is proud of four sons, and eight grandchildren.

When and where possible, he points others towards Christ.

Cornwall, 2022

Lightning Source UK Ltd.
Milton Keynes UK
UKHW020856010223
416292UK00006B/15